CONTENTS

THE WISDOM OF THE BUDDHA

Jean Boisselier

The 6th century BC, when the Buddha and his religion made their appearance, was a time of intense spiritual activity across all of Asia, from the easternmost parts of Greece to China. In India, the turmoil had begun even earlier. There, early in the second millennium before Christ, speculation about the cosmic order, self-knowledge and the destiny of beings had captured the collective imagination.

CHAPTER 1

INDIA IN THE BUDDHA'S DAY

According to Buddhist cosmography, the mythical Lake Anavatapta, located in the Himalayas, is considered the source of the four rivers that water regions populated by lions, bulls, horses and elephants. It will be the last lake to disappear – and the first to reappear – when the world, once destroyed, is reborn. The Ganges River is depicted running southwards (opposite).

The Hindu myth of the creation of the universe tells of the god Vishnu reposing on the cosmic waters and meditating about the world (right). During the course of his meditation there surges forth from his navel a golden lotus, from which emerges the god Brahmā, creator of the new universe.

It is impossible to imagine the rise of any spiritual movement outside a particular historical setting. Certainly, one cannot discuss the Buddha and early Buddhism without first placing oneself within the social and religious landscape of 6th-century BC India.

India before the 6th century BC

Despite long-established traditions of indigenous pre- and protohistorical societies, starting in the middle of the 2nd millennium BC, the culture and thought of the inhabitants of the Indian subcontinent began to be shaped by Aryan invaders. These peoples – generally presumed to have originated within the Caucasus (the area between the Black and Caspian seas) and to have migrated eastwards – first settled in

The Indus civilization of the 3rd millennium BC, the most ancient in the Indian subcontinent, occupied what is now the country of Pakistan, as well as southern Afghanistan and the Indian provinces of Punjab, Rajasthan and Gujarat. It is often divided into three stages:

pre-Indus (from the 4th millennium to around 2300 BC), Indusian (2300 to 1750 BC) and post-Indus (1750 to 1000 BC). It is not known whether its sudden disappearance was due to natural causes or to the Aryan invasion from the west. It shares several features with Mesopotamia, and is remembered chiefly for its urban, defensive and commercial systems (harbour basins and docks) and its roads. A reconstruction of Mohenjo-Daro, an important Indus settlement, is shown on the left. Neither the ceramics found there (an example, opposite) nor the seals bearing enigmatic inscriptions and decorations (above and left) have provided any clues about the religious practices.

the Indus River basin (in present-day Pakistan), driving back, subjugating or assimilating the aboriginal inhabitants. Towards the beginning of the 1st millennium BC, they reached the Ganges River basin in northeastern India. There, after fierce struggles that would inspire the writers of ancient India's renowned body of epic literature, they founded many kingdoms.

Aryan culture was based on a group of ancient texts and hymns that were held to be divinely revealed. These are known as the Vedas (*veda* meaning 'knowledge' in Vedic, the archaic form of Sanskrit). In addition to the Vedas are commentaries on the Vedic ritual tradition that, to the modern reader, reveal many aspects of ancient Indian society. First among these is the division

of society into four castes, a hierarchical system that, while officially banned by the Indian Constitution in 1949 (when India became a federal republic), still continues to some extent today. The first three castes, originally comprised exclusively of the conquering Aryans, invite comparison to medieval societies based on guilds. First was the priestly caste, the *brāhmans*; second, the warrior-nobles, the *kshatriyas*; and third, the merchants, farmers or herders, the *vaiśyas*. The fourth caste, the servants, or *śūdras*, was made up of indigenous peoples and fallen members of the first three classes.

Vedic beliefs: Brahman and Ātman

Within this societal framework, in around 1000 BC and later, religion was the exclusive domain of the brāhmans. Ritualistically oriented, their worship was based on sacrifice and involved prayers and offerings, sacred fire providing the link between the officiant and the divine. Like the gods of ancient Greece, the Vedic gods mingle with humans and intervene in human affairs. Numbering thirty-three, with the warrior-god Indra at their head, these are astral, terrestrial and aerial divinities, as well as such fundamental necessities of the sacrificial ceremony as the fire, the oblations, the practitioner and the sacrifical spot.

Among the future chief gods of Hinduism, one had already gained a prominent position: Brahmā (or, rather, Brahman). An impersonal god, he represents the

Agni, a Vedic fire divinity, is portrayed on the left with two heads in the company of his mount, the ram.

The Vedic god Indra is known for his lasciviousness and his tendency to drunkenness. Often provided with a third eye, at times (as in this mural, detail opposite) he is shown with numerous ones.

In this 17th-century miniature (below), a brāhman prepares himself to perform the *pūjā*, an act of worship of a divinity, involving sprinkling water on the idol, offerings and appropriate homages.

Universe, or the Word, with which the individual soul, the *ātman,* seeks to identify itself. In the Vedic tradition, relations with the gods were limited to supplications, never thanksgivings. They were established through prayer and, especially, through sacrifice, which ensured the bond between sacred and profane. During sacrificial ceremonies, priests acted both as representatives of the divinities in question and as proxies for the supplicant.

The emergence of Brahmanism

Once the Aryans reached the Ganges basin – and perhaps on account of their contact with indigenous cultures there – Vedic pantheistic notions began to evolve towards Brahmanism, 'an ensemble of religious and social conceptions defined and orchestrated by the brāhmans and forming a sacerdotal corpus' (Etienne Lamotte). Society and its institutions were regulated by the rules provided by the Vedas, which, taken as a whole, constituted the *dharma*, the order, or law, that determines all things. The brāhmans, while preserving Vedic rituals and sacrificial practices, took elements of religious beliefs about gods that were the object of local cults and integrated them into the Vedic pantheon – keeping their essence but modifying them to fit into this new context. From then on, in the foreground figured Vishṇu and his multiple 'descents' (avatars), Śiva and his various aspects, and, frequently, Brahmā. But also making their appearance were earth gods, spirits and demons – either in the service of, or enemies of, the gods. These included fabulous beings, such as *nāgas* (half-man, half-serpent guardians of riches) and *gandharvas* (celestial musicians with the head and upper

Borrowing from Buddhist art of the 2nd century BC, this winged figure (left) bearing offerings and depicted in a position of flight represents a heavenly being, or a 'bearer of learning' propitious to humans.

The Nāga (opposite, right), part man, part serpent, generally inhabits water and guards treasures and riches. Ancient Khmer (Cambodian) art gave the Nāga a prominent role, using its animal aspect to create a decorative element.

In Khmer temples of the first half of the 10th century, Brahmā (a sandstone sculpture, opposite) played a much more important part than the creator-god described in the Vedas. In one conception of the Brahmā–Śiva–Vishṇu trinity – according to which Śiva, supreme, occupies the centre – Brahmā was believed to have emerged from Śiva's right side, while Vishṇu issued from the left. Vishṇu is depicted on the left reposing on the many-headed serpent Ananta.

body of a human and the lower body of a horse or a bird); *yakshas*, attendants to Kubera, god of riches; *rākshasas* (the counterparts of the *yakshas*), attendants to the *asuras,* the gods' enemies; and other disconcerting beings, including ghosts and larvae.

The nonconformists of the 6th century BC

The pre-Buddhist spiritual landscape was peopled with numerous sages – some brāhmans, some not – who sought a resolution to the enigma of existence. Abandoning the world and worldly considerations, they were called 'renunciants'. Often they were solitary, itinerant, mendicant monks. Many, seeking only their own psychic advancement and the mastery of self, followed the practice of asceticism. This extremely ancient discipline – which is mentioned in the Vedic texts and which may have been indigenous to India – endeavours to control vital functions and needs. Initially adhering to the principles of brāhmanic life, ascetics moved beyond them in their quest to acquire supernatural powers, which included, for example, the ability to produce 'internal heat' (*tapas*) and to fall at will into ecstatic trances.

Other seekers of the truth, including the two masters chosen by the future Buddha, practised yoga. Through exercises that helped to give control over one's body and through meditation – not necessarily with any particular religious focus –

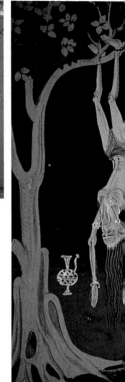

In contrast to Buddhist monks, with their ochre or yellow-coloured garb and shaved heads, 'renunciants' kept their hair in chignons and wore beards (above left).

This 7th-century sculpture from Mahābalipuram (left) is marked by a tremendous gentleness that reveals the moral ascendancy of the ascetic.

this discipline also led to spiritual mastery and the elimination of material desires and obstacles.

Another doctrine on the fringe of religion was Sāṃkhya (from a Sanskrit word meaning 'enumeration'), an analytic exposition of the twenty-five realities of which, according to ancient Indian philosophy, all things are composed – the first being Nature (*prakriti*), the last being the Individual (*purusha*), a spiritual entity. While the Buddha's tenets were developed partially in reaction to this and other similarly conservative traditions, echoes of Sāṃkhya doctrine can be found in Buddhism, although this school was not fully developed until the classical period, well after the beginning of the Christian era.

On the fringe of religious doctrines, yogis developed their spiritual powers by drawing from a whole collection of techniques, including Hatha-yoga ('yoga of effort'), in which movements and postures involve both the will and widely diverse muscular exertions. Here, yogis accomplish several yoga postures.

According to Buddhist cosmography, Lake Anavatapta is surrounded by five chains of mythical mountains, amongst which is Gandhamādana, a paradisiacal region inhabited by all sorts of marvellous beings. There one encounters the Buddhas who, being 'Enlightened for themselves alone', and thus not yet able to communicate the wisdom they have acquired, can reach only a provisory nirvāṇa. Ultimate nirvāṇa can be attained only with the emergence of the 'perfectly and completely Enlightened' Buddha. Awaiting the Buddha's arrival, these Buddhas sojourn together in this place. For purification ceremonies, performed according to the phases of the moon, they gather at a special spot at the foot of a tree famous for its extraordinary fragrance. The meeting hall nearby symbolizes 'the seats that always await them', referred to by Buddhist texts. Perfect understanding reigns in this paradise, in which beings manifest only friendly feelings towards one another. Horses and elephants are here distinguishable by their often unexpected colouring, which serves to identify their individual qualities.

The destiny of beings

No doubt born of the meeting of such animist conceptions and the empirical awareness of a natural evolutionary cycle and seasonal rhythms was the notion of death being followed by rebirth. This Vedic tradition of an endless migratory cycle is summed up in the notion of *samsāra,* according to which rebirth takes place within a social, or even animal, condition that has a relationship to one's actions in a prior existence. Following this logic, one faces eternal retribution for one's merits and faults. With the disappearance of the body at death, it is one's *karma* – the accumulation of moral acts in the last and previous lives – that determines one's state of rebirth.

From this unavoidable cycle of death and rebirth there was only one way out: the definitive integration of the individual soul with the realm of Brahman. As this release was restricted to only very exceptional beings, a new theory was born that clearly extolled the virtues of the acquisition of wisdom and the study and practice of asceticism; for those who did otherwise, death would be followed ineluctably by rebirth.

The Buddha, through his teachings, provided the long-hoped-for resolution to the question of a being's future. Without contradicting existing belief systems, he revealed a path of deliverance that was, for the first time, accessible to all.

The world and the universe

The spatial organization of the Buddhist world holds many similarities to the Vedic and Brahmanic cosmographies.

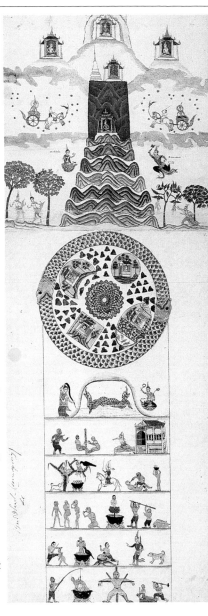

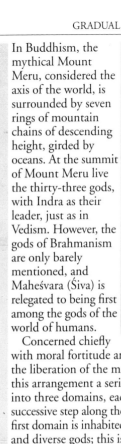

In Buddhism, the mythical Mount Meru, considered the axis of the world, is surrounded by seven rings of mountain chains of descending height, girded by oceans. At the summit of Mount Meru live the thirty-three gods, with Indra as their leader, just as in Vedism. However, the gods of Brahmanism are only barely mentioned, and Maheśvara (Śiva) is relegated to being first among the gods of the world of humans.

Concerned chiefly with moral fortitude and discipline leading to the liberation of the mind, Buddhism adds to this arrangement a series of worlds organized into three domains, each attesting to a successive step along the path of liberation. The first domain is inhabited by animals, humans and diverse gods; this is the earthly realm, with hells below and above a 'world of deities', the six levels of which manifest a being's increasing detachment from material desires. In the second domain, one finds only beings born in the realm of Brahmā; already liberated from desires, these beings divide themselves among four stages and seventeen levels, corresponding to the actual degree of liberation the spirit has attained. Beyond that is the third domain, the realm of the immaterial. *Nirvāṇa* ('extinction') – a cessation that does not signify nothingness but the absence of all that is, materially or spiritually – has no localization.

Mahākāla, originally an attendant of the god Śiva, in 10th-century Tantric Buddhism became a tutelary god and one of the eight 'guardians of the Law' – hence, his terrifying appearance in this 18th-century Tibetan painting (above).

In this representation of the Universe according to Buddhist cosmography (opposite) are depicted underground worlds and hells (towards the bottom) and the World of Desire and the various stages of the World of Appearances (towards the top).

The life of the historical Buddha is indissociable from legend. In it, the marvellous and the factual constantly intermingle, as do the sacred and the profane, and heavenly and earthly geographies. Before attaining 'perfect and complete Enlightenment', the Buddha was a Bodhisattva (literally, 'a being destined for Enlightenment').

CHAPTER 2

THE BODHISATTVA

Painted in the 6th century in the Ajantā caves in India, this figure (opposite) probably represents a principal Bodhisattva of Mahāyāna Buddhism. If the exact identity of the figure is unknown, it is still one of the most remarkable evocations of the ideals of grandeur and benevolence that characterize saviours.

During four outings he made in his father's pleasure gardens (right), the Bodhisattva encountered grim realities that had hitherto been hidden from him.

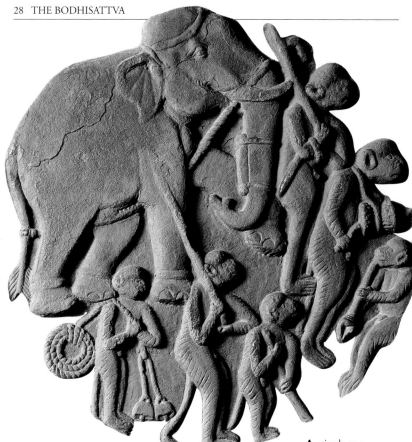

Distant events

For Buddhists – and for many others who, holding that
acts have good or evil consequences, believe in the transmigration of beings – the life of Siddhārtha Gautama,
the historical Buddha, was but the perfection of the long
moral evolution of a Bodhisattva, terminating in the rare
state of a 'perfectly and completely Enlightened' Buddha.

The edifying career of the Bodhisattva is conveyed to
us in two texts from the Pāli canon (Pāli being the
language in which the earliest Buddhist laws and stories
were transcribed in the 1st century BC). These two works,

A nimals are a
common feature
in 2nd-century BC
illustrations of the
Jātakas. Above: an
elephant being led by
monkeys.

In the teachings of
Hīnayāna Buddhism,
Maitreya (opposite
above), the Buddha
of future times, resides
among the Tushita gods,
the 'perfect ones'.

the Buddhavaṃsa (describing the lineage of the Buddha) and the Jātakas (stories about the previous lives of the Buddha), purport to relate tales told and statements made by the Buddha himself. Their popularity, especially that of the Jātakas, is revealed by the abundance of ancient visual depictions – including many from the middle of the 2nd century BC found in Bhārhut, in northern central India, before the stories existed in written form. It has not lessened since.

From Dīpaṅkara to Gautama: the Buddhavaṃsa

The mythical Buddhavaṃsa chronicles the lives of the twenty-four Buddhas who preceded Gautama and heralds the Buddha to come in the future – Metteyya (in Sanskrit, Maitreya). The text also identifies the beginning and, in particular, the unfolding of the career of the Bodhisattva himself. According to the Buddhavaṃsa, long ago, during the lifetime of a former Buddha named Dīpaṅkara, the first of the Buddha's predecessors, Gautama was a brāhman named Sumedha who led the life of an ascetic. One day, finding himself in the presence of Dīpaṅkara, he promised himself that he, too, would one day attain the state of Buddhahood. And Dīpaṅkara, because he was invested with the powers of clairvoyance belonging to all-knowing Buddhas, was able to assert to a crowd of listeners that, indeed, Sumedha 'would become a Buddha in this world'. This prediction was confirmed by each of the twenty-three intervening Buddhas, Dīpaṅkara's successors, while the future Buddha was reborn a multitude of times as a brāhman, a king, a yaksha leader, a Nāga, even a lion and other animals.

The brāhman Sumedha lays his hair under the feet of the Buddha Dīpaṅkara so that he will not soil his feet during his walk (left). By this act of humility and faith, he pledges to become the Buddha of the historical era, Gautama.

The 547 birth stories: the Jātakas

Enjoying a completely different kind of popularity, the Jātakas early on formed part of the foundation of Buddhist religious instruction and were not infrequently even better known by the faithful than were the main facts of the Buddha's life. The Pāli canon brings

A narrow, dark corridor within the wall of a 14th-century sanctuary in Sukhothai, Thailand, allows access to the level of the head of a colossal statue of the Buddha. The ceiling of the hallway is made up of a hundred engraved slabs (left, detail). The illustrations of the Jātakas that decorate them serve to guide the meditations of the devotees ascending this somewhat difficult route. On the left is a detail showing the Bodhisattva born as the horse of the king of Benares, who, at the point of death, pleads with the king for the pardon of his assailants.

These details (left and opposite) from an early 19th-century Thai painting illustrate the climactic moment of the Sāma Jātaka, one of the ten 'Great Jātakas'. In this story, the Bodhisattva, as Sāma, was the son and sole support of a couple of blind ascetics. One day, while bringing his parents water, Sāma was passing through a forest with a tame deer. He was spotted by a Benares king who was hunting in the same woods. Believing Sāma to be a supernatural being, he shot him with a poisoned arrow. Only acts of supreme faith brought Sāma back to life.

together the 547 tales of the previous births of the Bodhisattva, partitioned into twenty-two sections (theoretically based on the number of verses contained in each of the stories). Stanzas attributed to the Buddha, which accompany the tales, constitute a kind of short sermon intended for the listener's reflection. Each of the tales ends with a brief statement in which the Buddha links the identities of his contemporaries – friends or foes – with the various actors in the episode related, emphasizing in this way how one's moral inclinations, beneficent or evil, condition the trans-migrating being.

The ten sublimated virtues

One of the reasons the Jātakas hold such an esteemed and popular place in the Buddhist canon is that they describe the Bodhisattva's moral evolution. As is true of all beings – human, animal, or divine – on the path towards Enlightenment, the Bodhisattva was committed to the practice of a specific group of fundamental virtues, the *pāramitās*. The enumeration of these virtues differs slightly between the doctrines of the Buddhism 'of the ancients', known as Hīnayāna ('Lesser Vehicle'), and the more evolved Mahāyāna ('Greater Vehicle'), which emerged around the beginning of the Christian era.

In the ancient Buddhism of the Pāli canon, the pāramitās are described thus : acts of liberal giving,

It was not real life but Thai dance theatre that inspired the design of the figures in this painting. The wounded Sāma (opposite below) is wearing customary ascetic garb. The stance and gestures of the king (below) are those required by rules of traditional Thai dance for anyone drawing a bow.

morality, abnegation and renunciation, intelligence or wisdom, energy, patience and forbearance, truthfulness, determination, benevolence and equanimity. In Mahāyāna Buddhism, the act of giving and morality are given the same high rank. Different classifications are given to patience, energy and wisdom, and these are completed by five particular pāramitās: meditation, the mastery of means, determination, morality and knowledge. These extremes are selected as a function of Mahāyānistic doctrinal orientation. Be that as it may, both schools accord supreme importance to the act of offering; both regard it in a way that incorporates the worth of the giver and the receiver as well as that of the intention; and both recognize that, by its very nature, giving frees the giver from all attachments.

Boundless giving

For centuries, it has been from the Mahānipata (the 'large section', a reference to the number of stanzas of these texts in the Pāli canon) that the greatest borrowing has occurred. Each of these Jātakas is presented as a historical legend illustrating a virtue: abnegation, renunciation, energy, benevolence, determination, patience, morality, equanimity, honesty, intelligence and wisdom. The most famous Jātaka is the Vessantara Jātaka (number 547), an exaltation of the act of giving at its most extreme. Here, the Bodhisattva

The two most popular Bodhisattvas in the Mahāyāna faith are shown here (left) in two quite distinct traditions. Far left: an 8th- or 9th-century Khmer bronze statue of Maitreya. Near left: Avalokiteśvara seated in a posture of 'royal relaxation', an 11th- or 12th-century work from the Ta-li kingdom of south China.

was born as Prince Vessantara (Viśvāntara, in Sanskrit), son of the king of the land of Sivi. At the age of eight, Vessantara made a vow to make great donations, and in his life he fulfilled this pledge beyond all expectations.

At the age of sixteen, Vessantara married the princess Maddī, herself equally given to meritorious acts. Together they had two children. Soon, in compliance with the request of eight brāhmans, Vessantara gave away his white elephant. (This was no small sacrifice, as white elephants were regarded as the guarantors of the kingdom's prosperity.) This act led to the people's banishment of the prince and his family. Before leaving, however,

Artworks depicting the Jātakas often provide interesting details about daily life at the beginning of the Christian era. Above is an illustration of the Mahājanaka Jātaka, a lengthy tale about a prince, that shows some of the amenities of court life around the 6th century in India.

Executed on fabric at the beginning of the 19th century, this Thai painting (left) illustrates an episode of the Vessantara Jātaka. It depicts the moment when – brāhmans having claimed Vessantara's four horses – gods assume the guise of deer to replace them.

Vessantara distributed the remainder of his property – considered the supreme gift – yet he was also asked to surrender his four horses and his carriage. Forced to carry their children in their arms, the prince and princess arrived at the agreed-upon spot for their exile, where two retreats had been built for their use by the gods' master builder. But their trials did not end there; four months later, Jūjaka, an old and disreputable brāhman, came to demand Vessantara's children to be used as slaves for Jūjaka's young wife. This gift of one's own offspring, a gift superior to all others, could not be refused. Vessantara performed the proper rites and gave

Jūjaka his two children. The couple had to endure one more test. This time the gods demanded Maddī. Indra, disguised as a brāhman, made the request. But, revealing his identity at the very moment the gift was to take place, he returned Maddī to Vessantara and rewarded the prince by granting him eight wishes. Meanwhile, the king of Sivi was able to buy back his grandchildren from Jūjaka, who then died in a state of debauchery. At last able to return to their home, Vessantara and Maddī reentered the capital attended by a magnificent cortege, and Vessantara was crowned king and continued his acts of generosity.

The end of their trials. The children of Prince Vessantara were repurchased by the king, their grandfather, from the unworthy brāhman who earlier had demanded them as a gift. The exiles were led back with great ceremony into the capital, and there was such joy when the long-lost loved ones were reunited (below) that the earth shook. An earthquake and a tempest occurred, as they would at each of the major events in the Buddha's life. Below, the anonymous artist has suggested the characters' emotions by making use of the traditional hand gestures of Thai theatre.

The next-to-last existence

Following his death, Vessantara was reborn in Tushita Heaven (the realm occupied by the *tushitas,* the 'calm' or 'joyful' gods, the fourth of the six 'domains of desire'). All Bodhisattvas are born in Tushita Heaven for their

In this bas-relief (left) the Bodhisattva teaches the Law to the other gods in Tushita Heaven while awaiting the moment of his descent among humans for his final birth. The scene is depicted with great sobriety and a consummate knowledge of composition. It is a good example of 9th-century Buddhist art from Central Java.

On this fragment of a balustrade of a 3rd- or 4th-century Indian stūpa (a memorial shrine dedicated to the Buddha), a sculptor has depicted the descent of the Bodhisattva for his ultimate incarnation on earth in three juxtaposed scenes filled with a multitude of figures. On the left, the Bodhisattva is taking leave of the Tushita gods, consoling them by announcing that Maitreya will teach them the Law. In the central section is depicted his departure. He is seen as a white elephant, borne along in a procession under a canopy, with gods and goddesses of all ranks displaying their happiness. On the right, finally, is shown the premonitory dream of Queen Māyādevī, shown lying on her left side surrounded by her retinue, as she is always depicted in the art of Amarāvatī. The ensemble of compositions is strikingly faithful to both the letter and spirit of the *Lalitavistara,* the celebrated Sanskrit text from around the 1st century BC that relates the life of the Buddha.

penultimate existence, an existence that lasts an extremely long time as, according to canonical text, four hundred years in our world represents but a day in Tushita Heaven, and their life span lasts four thousand of their own years.

When the time comes for a Buddha to appear on earth, the gods 'of the ten thousand worlds' gathered together to ask the Bodhisattva to be born for his final existence among humankind. As it had been for the Buddhas of the past and will be for those of the future, they asked Svetaketu ('white and brilliant apparition', the Bodhisattva's name among the Tushita gods) to prepare to be reborn among humankind. Before having attained the end of their divine life – a moment whose prefiguring signs are obligingly set forth in Buddhist cosmological treatises – Bodhisattvas are called upon to prepare themselves for the ultimate birth, during which they will experience 'complete Awakening'.

So begins the biography of the historical Buddha

After extensive mental examinations, the Bodhisattva himself determined the most propitious time, continent, place of birth, lineage (clan), even the mother who would bear him. The knowledge that he had of past and future

events led him to choose, for a people, a modest confederation led by the Śākyas (a warrior clan) and, for parents, King Śuddhodana and his first wife, Queen Māyādevī. The Bodhisattva was now prepared to undergo any and all trials that ultimately would lead him to the 'attainment of Enlightenment' (the 'Awakening') and culminate in his being able to teach the Dharma, or 'Good Law', sought by all beings.

Having established his choices, the Bodhisattva expounded 'the eight hundred luminous doors of the Law' to the Tushita gods to 'instruct, enlighten, delight and comfort' them. He also introduced them to Maitreya, the Buddha of future times, who lives among them. All aspects thus having been settled, the Bodhisattva took leave of Tushita Heaven to be born among humans.

Siddhārtha's conception and birth

All texts generally agree on the basic story of the Buddha's earthly existence. Nevertheless, it is always highly embellished with the elements of the supernatural from which it is inseparable. It bears witness as much to the faith of the storytellers as to the tendency to magnify acknowledged facts – completely in conformity with the finest literary traditions of the Indian world.

The father and mother of the future Buddha were rulers of the modest Śākya tribe, a warrior caste whose founder was the brāhman Gautama (hence Siddhārtha's clan name). They lived in the principality of Kapilavastu,

'The Bodhisattva set about leaving the dwelling of the Tushitas. And, as he was departing, a light was projected from his body such that, by this light, this region of the world made up of three thousand great thousands was completely filled with a light surpassing the divine light, abundant, spread everywhere, one that had never appeared before.'

The Lalitavistara
Chapter v

in a region that is today southern Nepal. As King Śuddhodana and Queen Māyādevī were without children and had practised abstinence, the conception of the Bodhisattva was believed to be immaculate. One night in a dream, Queen Māyādevī saw a white elephant penetrate her side. For the soothsayers, this was a sign of the birth of a son who would be either a Universal Monarch (*cakravartin*) or – if he renounced the world – a Buddha. Ten lunar months after the conception, the queen, wishing to visit her parents, left Kapilavastu accompanied by her younger sister and her female attendants.

Māyādevī's dream is depicted on this medallion from Bhārhut (at the site of an imposing stūpa built in the 2nd century BC) in a relatively realistic fashion (below). The elephant is large, which indicates that this is not a depiction of an incarnation of the Buddha but rather Māyādevī's premonitory dream. Left: the 'Circle of One Thousand Rays of Light', a phenomenon that marked the departure of the Bodhisattva from Tushita Heaven.

'The capital is vanquished and in ruins,' noted the Chinese Buddhist pilgrim Hsüan-tsang, who visited Kapilavastu (left) at the beginning of the 7th century. (He clearly had confused the remains of a monastery there with the royal palace. In fact, nothing is left from King Śuddhodana's reign.)

During a stop in Lumbinī Park (just over the present-day Nepal-India border), the queen grasped a branch of a tree and gave birth to the Bodhisattva, who emerged from her right side without injuring her. The gods Indra and Brahmā took the young Bodhisattva into their arms – 'before he could be touched by human hand' – and cleansed him. Standing upright on a large lotus flower that had miraculously sprung from the site of his birth, the Bodhisattva was bathed again by two Nāga kings. Then, taking seven steps towards each one of the cardinal points, he proclaimed 'like a lion free of fear and terror' that he would vanquish 'sickness and death'.

From the heavens to the hells, the whole world celebrated the event. The Bodhisattva's future wife, groom and horse, as well as various kings, were born at the same moment. Seven days after the birth, Māyādevī died and was reborn in Tushita Heaven. Mahāprajāpatī, her younger sister, the king's second wife, would raise the Bodhisattva until he reached the age of seven.

The Buddha lived in the middle basin of the Ganges in the central zone of Uttar Pradesh. Kapilavastu, his birthplace, is in southern Nepal.

The seer Asita's prediction

Accompanied by the gods, the Bodhisattva was soon taken back to Kapilavastu with pomp and ceremony.

Taken away by the gods 'before he could be touched by human hand', the Bodhisattva (opposite below) stood upright on the ground and, knowing that he had arrived at his final birth, took seven steps towards each of the cardinal points in succession.

In accordance with Śākya custom, he was presented in the temple of Abhaya ('fearless'), the clan's patron divinity. The king bestowed upon his son a personal name, Siddhārtha ('who obtains success and prosperity'), and seers cast the child's horoscope and examined the 'thirty-two bodily marks and the eighty signs of the great man' with which he was adorned and which testified to honours bestowed upon him in past lives. Indeed, all signs augured well for Siddhārtha to become either a Universal Monarch or a Buddha. The first path would satisfy his father, the king, who had no other heirs; however, the second would be to the benefit of all beings.

Until the end of the 4th century, the various sects of the Āndhra region (in southeastern India), the source of this bas-relief (above), pondered the question of how to represent the Buddha, an exceptional being, superior to both humans and gods. Should he be given a human appearance, or should he be represented symbolically? Should one show him after the Enlightenment, or start with his birth? Here, symbolism has prevailed. The presence of the newborn is suggested by the depiction, centre and above in the composition, of a parasol framed by two fly whisks, symbols of the presence of a prince.

As is often true in Tibetan painting, this work, a highly decorative composition, presents a synthetic vision of events. Numerous details recall texts of the *Lalitavistara*. On the right, Māyādevī, the Buddha's mother, extends her 'right arm resembling a lightning bolt' towards the tree that 'bends to greet her'. On the left, the Bodhisattva stands 'on the large lotus that appeared, thrusting up through the ground'. Above him are 'Nanda and Upānanda, both of them Nāga kings, displaying their half-bodies in the expanse of the sky, having brought forth two streams of hot and cold water to bathe him.... In the air, a rare parasol appears...and standing on the large lotus, he looks at the ten points in space with a lion's expression, with the look of a great man.' Then, turning to face each direction, the Bodhisattva took seven steps, marked by lotuses that spontaneously appeared. The 'precious dwelling' that for 'ten months' duration' had isolated him from maternal contact is received by the gods and 'brought to the realm of Brahmā'. The exaggerated length of the Bodhisattva's arms is one of the 'thirty-two bodily marks of the great man'.

Yaśodharā's marriage suitors had to undertake three tests, one of which was the drawing of a bow, a feat that the Bodhisattva easily mastered. Depicted in the Chinese manner (a painting on fabric from Tun-huang, in China, opposite), this test of strength and skill is famous throughout the ancient world.

•At that time, the great sage Asita [left] lived on the far side of the Himalayas, the king of mountains, in the company of Naradatta, the son of his sister. He was gifted with five supernatural faculties. At the birth of the Bodhisattva, he saw a number of marvels, prodigious events and miracles. In the sky, the sons of the gods, full of delight, ran hither and thither shaking their sashes. At this sight, he said, "Come, I must look around me." With his divine vision taking in all of India he perceived that, in a large city called Kapila, in the house of King Śuddhodana, a little prince had been born, shining with a hundred sacred splendours, praised throughout the universe and adorned with the thirty-two bodily marks of the great man.•

The Lalitavistara
Chapter VII

No sooner had he been born than the Bodhisattva, raising his right hand, proclaimed his primacy over the world: 'I will be he who walks before all laws that have virtue at their root.' This representation (below) appears to have been influenced by Chinese iconography; the cranial protuberance, always evident on the adult Buddha, is rare on the Bodhisattva as a child.

The revelation that the child would take the second path, becoming a 'perfectly and completely Enlightened' Buddha, came from a seer named Asita. Asita, who lived in the Himalayas, had learned of the birth of the Bodhisattva by means of his supernatural powers and had flown by magic all the way to Kapilavastu to worship the child. When he discerned that Prince Siddhārtha would attain supreme intelligence and 'turn the Wheel of the Doctrine', he bemoaned the fact that he was so old he would not live to witness these events.

The early years

From his birth to the age of seven, Siddhārtha was raised by his aunt Mahāprajāpatī and his nurses. Few details are known about this period other than the child's acquisition, during his seventh year, of 'the first stage of meditation', an event that occurred during the ceremony of the 'sacred furrow' (an important annual rite in the Indian and Indianized world) performed by the king. That same year, Siddhārtha began his 'formal' education, learning to master the 'sixty-four arts', spiritual disciplines as well as technical and athletic skills. The Bodhisattva made rapid progress and was soon accomplishing great wonders, occasionally even surpassing his teachers.

Marriage and the princely life

When Siddhārtha turned sixteen, the age of majority, the Śākya council decided it was time for the future sovereign to marry and suggested to the prince that he do so. Reflecting that all past Buddhas also had married, Siddhārtha decided he could not refuse and informed the council of the specific qualities he thought suitable in a prospective spouse. The royal chaplain himself took part in the search among the Śākya clan for a bride. Eventually, a woman who met every one of Siddhārtha's stipulations was found. Her name was Yaśodharā (she is

This late-19th-century portrayal of the bow-drawing competition from a monastery in southern Sri Lanka is quite different from the one from Tun-huang shown on the preceding page.

also sometimes referred to as Gopā, or Bimbā). Having picked her out from a crowd of young maidens, the prince 'won' her by triumphing over other contestants in a competition of athletic prowess. In particular, he successfully bent the bow of his grandfather Siṃhahanu, a weapon that no one else was capable of even lifting.

After the couple was married, the king – who feared that the early predictions about his son's future (as well as a recent dream he had had about an errant monk) would come true and that one day soon Siddhārtha would renounce the world – made many attempts to bind the Bodhisattva tighter to his earthly royal destiny, providing all manner of amenities for the pleasing of all five senses.

The Four Encounters and disgust for the world

Pleasure gardens were created by the king in order to protect Siddhārtha from glimpses of suffering. Yet it was these very gardens that were to reveal, or rather awaken, the haunting acknowledgment of suffering – both physical and moral, continuously renewed in successive existences – that the Bodhisattva felt in the course of his time.

●In this dwelling, the first of all those in which the Bodhisattva would sojourn, and, while he stayed in this noble dwelling, the best of all refuges…the conches, the drums, the kettledrums, the brass drums, the harps, the lutes, the tambourines, the cymbals and the flutes brought forth sounds agreeable in their harmony, their sounds that were varied and resounding with symphonies while he was awake; and the troupe of women with voices that were supple, sweet and lively kept the Bodhisattva awake with their enchanting harmonies and concerts.●

The Lalitavistara
Chapter XIII

On his way to each of the gardens, to the east he is said to have encountered first an old man, 'weakened' and 'scorned, without protection, unable to act'. The second encounter, to the south, was to take place when he met a sick man 'worn out', who had 'reached the threshold of death without protection, homeless and without shelter'. To the west he is said to have encounted a funeral procession heading for the funeral pyre. So, having encountered 'old age, illness and death, which are always linked one to the other', the Bodhisattva resolved to think about 'deliverance'. It appeared to him during his fourth encounter, when to the north he encountered an itinerant monk who, 'with inner tranquillity', went 'without attachment, without hatred, begging for alms'. It was then that Siddhārtha became convinced that the religious life, so extolled by wise men and entered into voluntarily by the most esteemed personages when they reach a ripe age, was 'useful to one's self and useful to other beings'.

The king, aware of these encounters and of the prince's reaction to them, staged even more festivities to distract his son.

However, even though a son,

In a free, almost familiar style of Chinese inspiration, the three scenes reproduced here show the Bodhisattva on horseback (above) leaving the palace and confronting three of the truths that hitherto had been kept from him: a decrepit and miserable old man (above left), a bedridden sick man (left), and a monk strolling serenely (opposite below).

The third of the Four Encounters, that of the corpse being taken to the funeral pyre, is treated here in a more classical style by a Tibetan painter (left). The Bodhisattva is represented not as a solitary stroller but as Prince Siddhārtha in his chariot, accompanied by his retinue.

Rāhula ('bond, tie'), was born to Siddhārtha and Yaśodharā at about this time, the prince had already made his decision to renounce the world. The sight of his female attendants (procured for his pleasure by his father) – several of whom had fallen asleep in unbecoming positions – filled him with loathing, whereas he regarded paternity only as a new source of attachment.

The momentous encounter with a monk possessing 'inner tranquillity' and begging 'without attachment, without hatred' takes place, as do the others, at the very gates of the city. The painter conveys in the simplest way the precarious nature of the pleasure gardens intended to protect the Bodhisattva from the sight of suffering.

Reinforced in his decision to break with the world by the sight of his 'pleasure women' asleep in postures of immodest abandon, the Bodhisattva looks at his wife and newborn son one last time (left) before joining his groom and his horse.

The Great Departure and renunciation of the world

Thus, on the night of his twenty-ninth birthday, the Bodhisattva abandoned his family. After briefly watching his slumbering wife and son, he secretly departed from the palace on his horse, Kanthaka, accompanied by his groom, Chandaka. The gods facilitated the Bodhisattva's flight by plunging the town's inhabitants into deep slumber, opening the town gates and carrying the horse's hooves to muffle the sound. And, just as they had at the time of the Bodhisattva's descent from Tushita Heaven, miracles occurred throughout the universe.

The prince headed southeast, travelling through three

small kingdoms. In spite of the opposition of Māra – a very powerful god, considered as both a tempter and the personification of evil and death – whose first manifestation would be made here, he soon reached the river Anomā. There, in affirmation of his choice, he cut off his hair (which the gods carried to Indra's heaven), exchanged his clothes with those of a hunter and sent back his groom, his horse and his other princely adornments to Kapilavastu, as testimony to the irrevocable change. Kanthaka died of sorrow and was reborn in Indra's heaven. Such an example of animal fidelity is not uncommon in Buddhist lore.

The fact that the Bodhisattva not only relinquished his princely attire and adornments but cut his hair (above) indicated he had decided to reject the privilege of his caste and enter the path of religious mendicants.

Until the 5th century, the 'Great Departure', the entry of the Bodhisattva into religious life, was regarded as a miracle. Its artistic representation is more or less fixed. The gods hold up the horse's hooves while the groom holds on to its tail. The attire and saddlery (left) recall late-19th-century Burmese theatre costumes.

Triumphing over the final obstacles, the Bodhisattva reached the end of his long quest. Having become a 'perfectly and completely Enlightened Buddha', in possession of the Four Noble Truths, he began to teach what he had discovered, the 'Good Law', for the salvation of all beings.

CHAPTER 3

THE ENLIGHTENMENT AND THE FIRST SERMON

Opposite: throughout the second week after the Enlightenment, the Buddha stood, on a lotus flower, with his hands crossed, contemplating 'without blinking his eyes' the Bodhi Tree (also represented in the bas-relief on the right) and the 'diamond', 'unshakable' throne that had appeared at the moment he affirmed his will to attain Enlightenment.

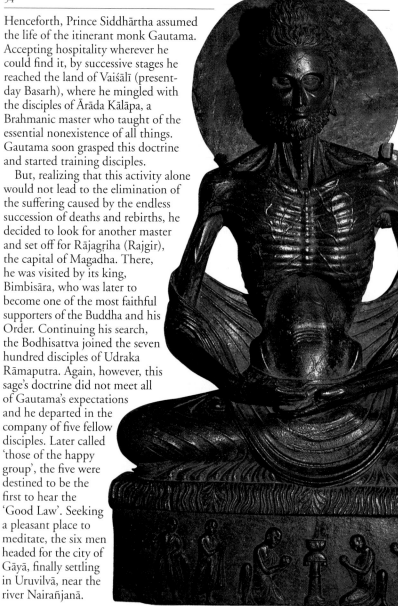

Henceforth, Prince Siddhārtha assumed the life of the itinerant monk Gautama. Accepting hospitality wherever he could find it, by successive stages he reached the land of Vaiśālī (present-day Basarh), where he mingled with the disciples of Ārāda Kālāpa, a Brahmanic master who taught of the essential nonexistence of all things. Gautama soon grasped this doctrine and started training disciples.

But, realizing that this activity alone would not lead to the elimination of the suffering caused by the endless succession of deaths and rebirths, he decided to look for another master and set off for Rājagṛiha (Rajgir), the capital of Magadha. There, he was visited by its king, Bimbisāra, who was later to become one of the most faithful supporters of the Buddha and his Order. Continuing his search, the Bodhisattva joined the seven hundred disciples of Udraka Rāmaputra. Again, however, this sage's doctrine did not meet all of Gautama's expectations and he departed in the company of five fellow disciples. Later called 'those of the happy group', the five were destined to be the first to hear the 'Good Law'. Seeking a pleasant place to meditate, the six men headed for the city of Gāyā, finally settling in Uruvilvā, near the river Nairañjanā.

The vanity of extreme asceticism

Not having found the hoped-for master, Gautama, now having become Śākyamuni ('sage of the Śākyas'), decided to try to discover the path to salvation himself. To do so, he, like many other sages in India, turned to practices and disciplines related to yoga, combining them with prolonged fasting. For six years, the gods watched as Śākyamuni wasted away and fell into a state of extreme weakness. Growing alarmed, they alerted his mother – who had been reborn among them – as well as his father, Śuddhodana. But the king, knowing that Siddhārtha's success had been prophesied by the gods, refused to believe that his son had not attained his goal and did nothing. Thus, the Bodhisattva continued in the same way until eventually even the 'bodily marks of the great man' vanished from him and his faculties grew weak. Māra, the personification of evil, whom Gautama had first met upon his decision to renounce the world, now reappeared. Māra (from the Sanskrit *mṛi*, 'death') is a very important god who rules over eleven stages of the World of Desires: four stages of unfortunate destinies (hells, animals, ghosts,

D ressed as a Buddhist monk, the Bodhisattva receives instruction from the Brahmanic master Udraka Rāmaputra on the production of a state neither conscious nor unconscious (left). Realizing, however, that this state could not lead to the Awakening that he sought, the Bodhisattva left and began to fast and to practise holding his breath, an exercise derived from Hatha-yoga ('yoga of effort'). His extremely gaunt figure is portrayed in this unidealized sculpture of the Gandhāra school (opposite) from the 2nd century AD. Such demanding asceticism weakened him to such a point that even his five companions became alarmed (below).

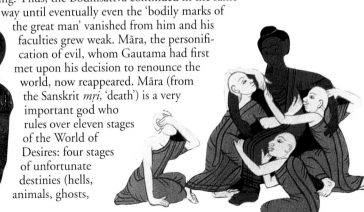

Asuras) and seven stages of fortunate destinies (humans and six stages of divinities who, in their quest to taste pleasures more and more ethereal, are no less bound to the satisfaction of the senses). Māra knew that if the underlying reason for the unending cycle of death and rebirth were discovered, his power would be ruined. Hence, he struggled to thwart the achievement of Gautama's goal.

At a point when Gautama's vitality had all but vanished, Indra suddenly appeared to him. Playing a three-stringed lute, the god showed Gautama that it is only a string properly tuned that can produce a pleasant sound, while one that is too slack gives no sound at all, and one that is too tight breaks. In the same way, he implied, only people who avoid all kinds of excess will attain the goals they set for themselves. Gautama decided therefore to end his life of useless asceticism. Still faltering, he undertook to restore his appearance and his power. From a cadaver's shroud (according to another version of the story, the rags of a dying woman) he fashioned himself a monk's garment and began

Hsüan-tsang, a 7th-century AD Chinese pilgrim, reported that the Bodhisattva waited in a cave beneath Mount Prāgbodhi (left) until a god revealed to him that he would attain Enlightenment only at the foot of the Bodhi Tree, several kilometres from there.

'Sujātā prepared, with cream collected from the milk of a thousand cows and with a handful of new rice, the most savoury and nourishing of foods…. It was this precious food that she brought him under the tree of the goatherd [below].'

The Lalitavistara
Chapter XVIII

The Bodhisattva throws the golden bowl into the river (opposite).

to beg for his subsistence in order
to regain his strength and attain the
Enlightenment he had been seeking
for six years. Villagers offered him food, and
he soon recovered his health and his faculties.

His five companions, however, did not
understand why Gautama had abandoned his
austere practices. He seemed to them to have
admitted defeat. They left him and departed
for Rishipatana, near Benares. The
Bodhisattva headed for the 'tree of the
goatherd' (*ajapāla*), under which he continued his
meditations. It was there that a young girl named
Sujātā ('well-born'), believing she was in the
presence of the divinity of the tree to which
she had made a wish, made an offering to
Gautama of succulent boiled rice in a golden bowl.

Preparation for the 'supreme, complete Awakening'

The previous night, the Bodhisattva had had five
premonitory dreams about the imminence of his

attainment of Enlightenment. Thus, after bathing in the river Nairañjanā, he divided the food he had received from Sujātā into forty-nine parts – one for each of the forty-nine days he now knew would be necessary for the consecration of the 'Awakening'. Then, because a monk is not allowed to keep any precious objects, Gautama threw the golden bowl into the river. It travelled upstream to the domain of the Nāga king Mahākāla and bumped against the three precious bowls that the three Buddhas who preceded Gautama had thrown under the same circumstances.

He spent the rest of the day in the nearest wood. Now having recovered all of the 'bodily marks of the great man', he knew that he was ready to attain Enlightenment and headed towards Bodhimanda ('site of Enlightenment'), the inalterable site considered to be the earth's centre and the only place capable of withstanding the weight of the Enlightenment that the successive Buddhas attain there. There he sat facing east on a scattering of sacred grass (*kuśa*) he had requested from a grass cutter.

According to the Commentary on the Jātakas, this was the beginning of the 'final and recent circumstances' during the course of which the Bodhisattva, through the 'full act of Enlightenment', becomes the Buddha who will teach the Four Noble Truths.

Assaults and defeat of Māra

Once again, the evil god Māra tried to interfere. Desperate to put an end to Gautama's endeavour, he sent a horde of demons to scare him. Māra was forced to admit defeat.

Since it is, in fact, the triumph of virtue over all the chains binding beings that permits the attainment of Enlightenment, this episode in the Bodhisattva's life is considered by Buddhists as the high point of his career. The necessity of illustrating this idea, using symbols accessible to everyone, explains the ongoing success of depictions representing the assaults and ultimate defeat of Māra.

The Buddha's right hand pointing to the ground evokes his victory over Māra (left and detail opposite).

The Bodhisattva's victory over Māra – and over all the forces of evil over which he rules as master of the worlds enslaved by desires – could only be depicted by means of allegory. To more effectively convince the faithful of the dangers with which they were threatened, written texts also used this approach. It is difficult to know whether the images inspired the texts or the latter guided sculptors and painters in the first manifestations of Buddhist art. To evoke the dangers, the most frightening and demonic figures were depicted. The same vocabulary has

The attainment of Enlightenment

According to tradition, it was during the night of the full moon of the month of Vaiśākha (April–May), on Gautama's thirty-fifth birthday, that he became the Buddha. During the first watch (in India, the nights are

been used in all regions where Buddhism is practised and in every era. Above left: a Chinese view of Māra's assaults.

divided into three periods, or 'watches'), the Bodhisattva
experienced the four successive stages of meditation that,
freeing his intellect from material concerns, led him to
'total purity of imperturbability and presence of mind'.
During the second watch, thanks to his powers of vision
(his 'divine eye'), he reflected on the unfolding of his

This colossal rock carving, executed in the 12th century at Polonnaruwa, Sri Lanka, shows the Buddha meditating.

prior existences and those of other beings. In doing so, he focused on the incessant and grievous repetition of beginnings and the resulting suffering. The 'supreme, complete Enlightenment' occurred during the third watch. Now fully conscious of the 'law of reciprocal origination' of causes and effects – numbering twelve – and their inevitable correlation, the Bodhisattva discovered by deduction how to put an end to the cycle.

Seated with his hands joined in his lap, the Buddha meditates. The sequence of ten of his predecessors in the same posture on the pedestal enables us to positively identify this statue of the 3rd or 4th century (left) as the Buddha Gautama. The same can be inferred from this painted Sri Lankan image of the 19th century (below), since only one Buddha attained Enlightenment under the pipal tree.

At this moment, he came into possession of the Four Noble Truths – the Truth about suffering; the Truth about the origin of suffering; the Truth about the cessation of suffering; and the Truth about the Eightfold Path (whose eight branches symbolize the acquisition of the eight perfections), which leads to the cessation of suffering – and thus became the Buddha.

This was the second great miracle. The gods – who, through Māra's evil efforts, had temporarily withdrawn – returned to celebrate the Buddha and wrought marvels appropriate to the occasion. These Truths were also the fundaments of a doctrine that was 'difficult to understand' that a 'supremely and completely Enlightened' Buddha had to teach. It revealed to the ensemble of beings the path allowing an end to transmigration, samsāra.

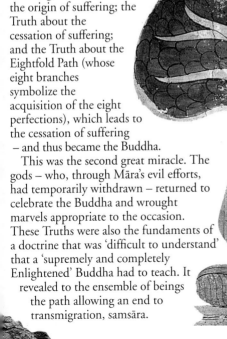

King Rāma III of Thailand (reigned 1824–51) launched a vast programme of construction and restoration of Buddhist temples, which allowed an exceptional expansion of mural painting in that country, including the paintings of Wat Thong Thammachat in 1850 in Thonburi, the town that faces Bangkok from across the river. While these may not count among the major paintings of this period, they nonetheless have a great deal of charm and interest, while adhering to traditional principles of classical Thai murals. The three scenes reproduced here and on the previous pages illustrate pivotal episodes from the Buddha's career. Pages 62–3: the god Indra, playing the lute, entreats the Bodhisattva to choose the middle path, the avoidance of excess, which is the only way to experience progress. Pages 64–5: Sujātā and her servant offer a bowl of boiled rice to the Bodhisattva seated under the 'tree of the goatherd'. Left: King Bimbisāra gives the hermitage in the Bamboo Grove to the Buddha and his nascent Order. As is the custom on such occasions, the gift is sanctified by water poured on the hand of the beneficiary by the donor.

It showed them that it is by refraining from sin and practising goodness and purity of thought that, through meditation, one arrives at the right knowledge, which leads to nirvāṇa, the ineffable state of nonrebirth.

The first weeks after Enlightenment

In traditional Buddhist lore (mainly Pāli texts) it is said that the Buddha remained on the site of his Enlightenment, or in the immediate vicinity of Bodhimanda, for seven weeks, during which time he practised meditation and various spiritual exercises.

The first week he spent under the Bodhi Tree (*aśvattha*, a pipal tree, or *Ficus religiosa*), in accordance with the law 'that forbids kings to leave the site of their consecration during the seven days that follow it' (Jean Filliozat), and meditated on the 'law of reciprocal origination', as all earlier Buddhas had done. During the second week, having confirmed to the gods the attainment of Enlightenment, he appeared northeast of the Bodhi Tree, in the region of Bodh-Gayā. Standing immobile, he contemplated it without

In the 3rd century BC, the Bodhi Tree was the object of a veritable cult begun by Aśoka, king of Magadha, India, who surrounded it with a galleried courtyard. When he introduced Buddhism to Laṅkā (modern Sri Lanka), a cutting of this tree was brought to that island. The original tree in India died in the 12th century. In about 1884, a cutting of the newer tree was brought back.

The 'footprints' of the Buddha are some of the most ancient objects worshipped by Buddhists. At Bodh-Gayā, a centre even more important for worshippers of Śiva and Vishṇu than for Buddhists, the footprints cannot always be attributed with certainty to one or the other of the two religions.

blinking for seven days' duration. During the third week, he repeatedly strolled from this point to the site of the Enlightenment – a distance of only about fifteen metres, according to the writings of Hsüan-tsang and archaeological discoveries (Alexander Cunningham). The *Lalitavistara* asserts that the path he took led up to the 'regions of the three thousand great thousands of worlds'. The framework of the fourth week, spent in meditation on the doctrine and the work ahead of him, was 'the abode of jewels' (*ratnagriha*), erected by the gods of the northwest. In the fifth week, the Buddha returned to the 'tree of the goatherd'.

Buddhists regard Mahābodhi, at Bodh-Gayā, the site of the Enlightenment, as the most important of all the pilgrimage sites. It is believed that all Buddhas, past and future, attain complete Enlightenment there after triumphing over Māra and the forces of evil. On the site of the present-day temple, Aśoka had a small sanctuary erected. A larger temple, whose construction is attributed by Hsüan-tsang to a Sri Lankan king, replaced it in the 5th or 6th century. Destroyed by Muslims in the 12th century, it was restored, rebuilt and modified on several occasions, principally by Burmese Buddhists, who gave it its present shape (left) and maintained it through subsequent restorations.

The Buddha is generally depicted seated on the coils of the Nāga Mucalinda, as if artists were repelled by the notion of direct contact between the serpent and the body of the Blessed One. Thus, although more faithful to the texts, this late Sri Lankan image (left) is unusual.

According to some accounts, Māra's three daughters intervened, but they were made to see the decrepitude that awaited them.

The Nāga Mucalinda

The Buddha spent the sixth week in a different kind of meditation, under the Mucalinda tree beside a lake of the same name. An unseasonal cold and rain might have interrupted his meditation or even threatened confirmation of the attainment of Enlightenment if Mucalinda, the Nāga of the lake, had not come to the rescue. Recalling that previous Buddhas had undergone the same trial – and eager to acquire merits – he protected the Blessed One by wrapping himself around his body and shielding him with his dilated hood. While difficult for Western minds to grasp, and almost totally ignored by some Buddhist sects, this prodigious event is nonetheless regarded by many others as irrefutable evidence of the attainment of

In Thailand, this unusual gesture of the Buddha evokes the act of Enlightenment in all its aspects, from the victory over Māra to the final meditation under Mucalinda's protection.

Enlightenment and has long been a popular theme, as the earliest examples of the visual arts in India (seen in sites in Bhārhut and Pauni) and, later, throughout Indianized southeast Asia bear witness.

During the seventh week, the Buddha proceeded to a spot beneath the Royal Site (*rājātana*) Tree. It was there, on the last day of the week, that Trapusha and Bhallika – two brothers from either Bactres or the Malay Peninsula – merchants from a passing caravan, offered him food. The guardian gods of each of the cardinal points at once presented him with four bowls made of precious materials from which to eat his meal. The Buddha, however, unable to take food in anything but a begging bowl, was obliged to refuse these gifts. Four stone bowls were then presented to him. Taking them, the Buddha fashioned them into a single bowl so that each of the gods would receive merit for his gift. Now that their offering of food

A return to normal life is marked by the Buddha's acceptance of food offered by the two merchants. The Thai painting below depicts the Buddha seated 'European fashion', a convention adopted for occasions when someone accepts a gift because it permits a posture of goodwill towards the gift giver – a slight inclination forwards. The Buddha holds a begging bowl that is similar to those used by Buddhist monks. In this painting, it is clear that the bowls given by the four gods of the cardinal points have already been accepted and cast into a single bowl.

could be accepted, the two merchants 'took refuge in the Buddha and the Dharma'. The Blessed One gave to his first converts nail parings and locks of hair – relics that, upon returning to their own country, the two would enshrine in a stūpa.

Can the Dharma be taught?

Returning to the 'tree of the goatherd', the Buddha mused on the teaching of the Doctrine, so necessary to all beings but also so difficult to grasp. If only he had a master in whom he could confide his indecision. Brahmā Sahampati then appeared before him and exhorted him to regard the Dharma as his master and urged him to conquer his hesitation.

The Buddha remained silent, but in his mind appeared an image that helped confirm his resolution. He saw a pond filled with lotus plants whose flowers were either so deeply immersed in the water that they would never reach the surface, or were already standing upright flowering in the full light, or were almost on the surface of the water. The Buddha could see that the first would never bloom, the second had already achieved their goal, and it would not take much for the last to blossom.

Similarly, he reasoned, people could be separated into three groupings: those who were prisoners of error and false teachings, those who had found the truth, and, finally, those still seeking the way. The first have not yet recognized the path, while the second were already upon it; neither one nor the other had need of instruction. There were throngs of those in the third

Depictions of the First Sermon are often identified by the presence of deer (from which the site, Deer Park, derives its name) surrounding the Wheel of the Law, its symbol. In theory, there were no other human listeners besides the five of 'the happy group', but several texts and images show that the gods who had insisted that the Law be taught also were assembled there to profit from the lesson, 'which enables self-guidance'. A 17th-century Tibetan depiction of the event is reproduced on the left.

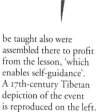

group – those who were hesitant about which path to take. The Buddha knew that the least amount of help could offer them salvation. Therefore, it was to them that he decided he would teach the Law.

Which listeners should be sought?

Who would be most likely to grasp the Teaching? The Buddha thought first of all of his former teachers, Udraka and Ārāda, but his all-seeing 'divine eye' told him that both had recently died. His thoughts turned to the five companions who had left him when he had renounced austerities, and he decided to join them near Benares, where they had gone. Arriving at the bank of the Ganges without the means to pay the fare for his passage across, he called on his supernatural powers (to which he resorted only on very rare occasions). Landing on the opposite bank, he continued on towards Deer Park (Mrigadāva, also called Rishipatana, 'site where [the ashes of] the ascetics fell'), where he found his former companions. Still not comprehending the Buddha's past 'reversal', the five

In India, the term 'lotus' signifies real lotuses as well as water lilies, distinguished only by their colours. Often serving as seats or supports for Buddhas and Bodhi-sattvas, they provide an essential element in pictorial narrations. Tantric Buddhism likens them to the heart 'in the city of the body' – the feminine sex – while lyric poetry endlessly exalts their beauty.

pretended to be unaware of his
approach. But as the Buddha drew
nearer, they began to feel ill at ease.
Forgetting their resolve, they arose to
meet the 'Reverend' (*āyushmant*)
Gautama, whom they welcomed and
complimented for the 'perfect mastery
of his senses and the clarity of his
complexion'. The Blessed One told
them he was no longer the 'Reverend'
Gautama but a *Tathāgata* (a term which
they evidently knew, but the meaning
of which is still discussed today – eight
or even sixteen varying interpretations
having been proposed by the
commentaries). The Buddha added that
he was 'omniscient, all-seeing, free of
impurities', and 'prevailed over all laws'.
He announced that he would teach the
Law and that they, the five of 'the happy
group', would be his first listeners.

The Benares Sermon

The Buddha's First Sermon, also known
as the Benares Sermon, was dedicated
to expounding the Four Noble Truths
and is often referred to as the 'Setting
in Motion of the Wheel of the Law'.
This expression appears in the 3rd-
century AD *Lalitavistara* and later in Pāli
commentaries. But the symbolism of the
wheel had asserted itself much earlier, as
it was customarily used to symbolize the
Good Law and the Teaching of

This gesture of the
Buddha (right and
detail above) commonly
signifies the First Sermon.

the Buddha in all ancient Buddhist iconography from
the reign of Aśoka to the 3rd or 4th century AD. The
symbolism is unequivocal; just as the solar disk illumines
the earth, the Wheel represents the Law of the Buddha,
the light of the world shining for all beings. It is the
Wheel (*cakra*), first among the treasures of the Universal
Monarch (*cakravartin*), that guides him. And one of his
principal attributes, according to the Buddhist

perspective, is to broadcast the Good Law 'for the good of all beings'.

At the announcement of the First Sermon, the third of Buddha's great miracles, the same marvels as had occurred on the two previous occasions – his birth and his Enlightenment – took place. It was the evening of the full moon of the month of Āshādha (June–July). During the first watch, the Buddha remained silent. During the second watch, he explained why excessive asceticism is to be avoided and why monks should turn away from extremes and seek 'the middle path'. Finally, during the third watch, he explained the Doctrine, the Good Law, that marked the beginning of the Teaching and, with the adherence of the first disciples to follow it, that of the Order (Saṅgha). Ājñāta Kauṇḍinya was the first of the five to grasp the scope of the Teaching, and upon his conversion he attained the status of an *arhant*, a saintly state leading to nirvāṇa. The four others would not reach that point until five days later, after hearing a sermon on impermanence and 'the nonself'. The Order thus having been established, the Teaching could now be delivered to all.

The Wheel of the Law, symbol of the Doctrine and its Teaching since Aśoka's reign, stopped being depicted in India in the 5th and 6th centuries. Curiously, it is only in the ancient kingdom of Dvāravatī (in the central and western regions of present-day Thailand) that, from the 7th to the 9th century, it maintained an unusual importance. Sometimes of large dimension (nearly two metres in diameter), it would often be set on top of a pillar and flanked by four deer, a classical allusion to the First Sermon. Some wheels, such as this 8th-century one (above), and certain pillars also bear inscriptions referring to the Doctrine.

Having decided to 'devote himself to the Law that he himself had discovered, to honour, respect and serve it', the Buddha was determined to spread the Teaching to the best of his ability; he believed that many people would be lost if they did not hear the preaching of the Law. He identified what would become one of the fundamental tenets of Buddhism – to make a gift of the Law.

CHAPTER 4

TEACHINGS AND PEREGRINATIONS

Two rather different gestures evoke the same concept: the Teaching dispensed untiringly by the Buddha over forty-five years. Opposite: a detail of a 5th- or 6th-century mural from ancient Afghanistan portraying him seated on a lotus in the so-called argumentation gesture. Right: a 3rd-century Indian bas-relief from Amarāvatī of the Buddha welcoming his listeners.

The Buddha was now in his thirty-sixth year. During the next forty-five years, until his Total Extinction, he travelled through the middle basin of the Ganges accompanied by his disciples, begging his daily food and spreading his Teaching without discrimination. Only the rainy season (from June/July to October/November), because the wet weather made movement so difficult, interrupted his journeys.

During these months, monks and laypeople alike could receive the Teaching at a site selected for retreat. It is said that it was during these occasions that the Jātakas were narrated by the Blessed One. The imposed sedentary retreats gave a locus and structure to the monastic life, but it should be pointed out that, not long after his Enlightenment, the Buddha also had sent monks off in all directions in an effort to spread the Doctrine as widely as possible, for the good of 'the greatest number'.

The progress of conversions

The five of 'the happy group' were already itinerant monks when they met he who would become the Buddha. Hence, the first lay-person to be converted and to enter the Order was Yaśas, the son of a Benares (now called Varanasi, in Uttar Pradesh) treasurer, who was disenchanted by the luxury and pleasures of his adolescence and ran away to 'take refuge in the Buddha, the Law, and the Saṅgha [the Buddhist monastic community]'. After finding their son among the monks, Yaśas' father and mother became the first lay followers (*upāsaka* and *upāsikā*).

Interestingly, the two travelling merchants who became

This cowherd and his animals (opposite), depicted in a cave painting from Qizil, in Central Asia, reminds the viewer that the Teaching is addressed to everyone and is intended to be understood by all.

Because of the special instruction they receive when they are admitted into the Order, monks are more easily able to grasp the scope of the Teaching, which they, in their turn, must disseminate. Seated on a lotus, surrounded by a flaming and haloed aura, the Buddha in an informal pose dispenses instruction (left, a 7th-century mural from Qumtura, in Central Asia).

Monks and disciples are often depicted in procession, hands joined in an attitude not of prayer but of respectful devotion (below).

the first converts may not even have been of Indian origin. Yaśas and his parents, although very rich, were nonetheless vaiśyas, that is, members of the common class. Soon, the addition of the barber Upāli, a śūdra (from the servant class), who would prove to be a major disciple, shows the degree to which Buddhism was established outside the caste system.

At the end of the rainy season, when the monks – already numbering about sixty – each left in various directions to preach, the Buddha returned to Uruvilvā. Along the way, he converted a group of thirty young revellers, urging them to 'go in search of themselves'.

Because of both the number and quality of the conversions at Uruvilvā – in particular, that of the three Kaśyāpa brothers – they took on new significance. As a result of the array of wonders the Buddha performed, conversions multiplied. They were particularly widespread following the delivery of the Fire Sermon, which was given near Bodh-Gayā, on the Gayāśīrsha hill. In this lesson, the Buddha showed that everything in the world is inflamed by passions and only those who follow the

Banners of fabric painted with didactic subject matter play an important role in Buddhist art, whether created in the ancient tradition or in the later, Mahāyāna, school. This banner (left), typical of 19th-century Thai art, depicts the Buddha in the *abhaya* posture, a gesture 'that calms, that reassures', also called the gesture of 'absence of fear' (a confusing term, as fear is an emotion that a Buddha would never feel in any situation). The central figure is framed by two of his greatest disciples, Śāriputra and Maudgalyāyana, always represented at his side in an attitude of adoration, symmetrically placed and leaning slightly forwards. In the heaven above are two divinities. These are understood to be always present, even when they cannot be seen. In the lower portion of the banner, three cups and two candles are arranged on a special offering table. The pig and the hare probably refer to the astrological cycle of twelve animals. The composition as a whole depicts an offering given in a temple to the indissociable trinity: the Buddha, the Law and the Saṅgha.

Eightfold Path (that is, right view, right resolve, right speech, right action, right livelihood, right effort, right mindfulness and right concentration) can achieve complete independence. Each person who heard it instantaneously attained the status of arhant.

The chief disciples

During his first trip to Rājagṛiha, before he had become the Buddha, Gautama had promised its king, Bimbisāra, that he would return to communicate the Truth to him once he had discovered it. Now, accompanied by his monks, he headed for the city, stopping in the southwest in the Stem Grove (Yashṭivana), the place of his first sojourn. Bimbisāra welcomed them and invited them for a meal in his palace the next day. After hearing a sermon, he and some other listeners became adherents. After the meal, the king put the Bamboo Grove

Notable because of the quality of the converted – the three Kaśyāpa brothers, for instance, were brāhmans who enjoyed great renown – the conversions that took place in Uruvilvā were also unusual in their magnitude. According to the texts, there were between 500 and 3500. On the left is a copy of a 19th-century mural from Bangkok depicting the Kaśyāpa brothers.

With the exception of Sānkāśya, further northwest, all the sites in which the Buddha's life and teaching took place were in the fertile middle basin of the Ganges (that is, in a region only slightly larger than England), an area as important for Brahmanism as for Buddhism. The confluence of the Ganges, the Yamunā, and the 'invisible Sarasvatī' rivers is regarded as the most sacred spot of all.

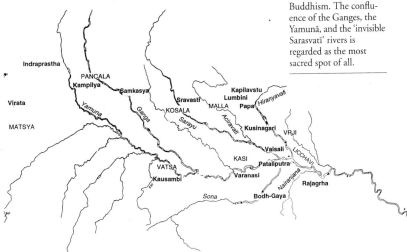

(Veṇuvana) at the disposal of the Buddha and his Order, who elected to remain for two months.

During this sojourn, a monk named Śāriputra became acquainted with one of the Buddha's disciples and, through him, with the essence of Buddhist doctrine. He decided to join the Order, bringing with him his friend Maudgalyāyana. (Until that point, both men had been leading disciples of one of the principal teachers of the day, Sañjayin, whom they tried without success to rally to the cause of the Buddha and his doctrine.) Premier among the Buddha's chief disciples, the two formed the Buddha's 'principal pair of listeners'. Soon the group in the Bamboo Grove was joined by the brāhman Pippali, also known by the name Mahākāśyapa, who had long been practising abstinence. After only three brief lessons from the Buddha, Pippali was ordained at Veṇuvana when he spontaneously prostrated himself at the Blessed One's feet. Pippali was the beneficiary of an extraordinary benevolence, a sign of the leading role he would later play.

The conversions became so numerous in Rājagriha that the Magadhians, fearing their social impact, became alarmed and began castigating the monks. The Buddha calmed everyone by assuring them that the problem would be of short duration and reminding them that nobody was being forced to join the Order.

Voyage to Kapilavastu

Although the Buddha's return to his home in Kapilavastu is not recorded in all the texts, when it is, it is said to have been in response to King Śuddhodana's request. No longer able to ignore his son's great renown, the king had sent nine messengers to him, one after the other – to no avail. All nine had joined the Order and

Variously represented in Buddhist art, halos and auras are directly related to the luminous manifestations said to be produced by the Buddha on all significant occasions. Above is a sculpture from the Indian school of Sārnāth. On the left is a detail from a Tibetan painting.

Among the 'thirty-two bodily marks of the great man', two of those concerning the hands and feet are, according to the Sanskrit list, the 'mark of a wheel' and the 'interdigital membrane' (opposite), frequently interpreted as a simple web related to palmistry.

remained in Rājagṛiha. Udāyin, son of the royal chaplain and childhood companion of the Blessed One, was the tenth envoy. He was also converted and entered the Order, but this time, the Buddha agreed to travel back to Kapilavastu, knowing his family would now be receptive.

Undertaken a little less than a year after the Buddha's Enlightenment, during the full moon of February–March, the trip lasted two months. Twenty thousand monks are said to have accompanied the Buddha. The king at first intended to greet his son publicly, but his pride was wounded when he saw the group of begging monks from whom the Buddha was indistinguishable. He changed his mind, however, when Udāyin made him understand that it was as glorious to be the father of the Buddha as it was to be the father of a Universal Monarch, as Śuddhodana had wished his son to be.

In the customary manner for a religious group, the monks settled outside the city, in the Banyan Grove. Out of pride of caste, the Śākyas at first refused to bow before the Buddha, a wandering monk, even though he was their own relative. So, in order to spare his father unnecessary embarrassment, the Buddha decided to

Bas-reliefs on the 1st-century BC stūpa of Sānchī (details above), in north-central India, refer symbolically to the Buddha's presence: the throne beneath the tree, footprints, the Wheel of the Law. The left-hand detail is a representation of the magical walkway the Buddha traversed in the presence of the Śākyas in Kapilavastu. The right-hand detail shows the flooding of the Nairañjanā. Victims of the flood, the Kaśyāpa brothers (in the boat), have abandoned their instruments of sacrifice, which drift away. The Buddha walks on the waves and causes his followers to convert *en masse*.

appear on an aerial walkway, thereby allowing the Śākyas to lift their eyes to him instead of having to bow before him. At the same time, he revealed his powers to them by performing the miracle of the 'double appearances'.

The next day, despite the Buddhist stipulation that one must beg for one's food – an act that scandalized his family – the principal Śākyas converted. First to do so was King Śuddhodana, the Buddha's father. Then came Nanda, his half brother, diverted by the Buddha from a marriage he

The man who was to become the omniscient Buddha left his wife and newborn son as they slept. Whether his wife had perhaps not lost hope of winning him back or whether she simply wanted to introduce him to his son, now six years old, she pushed the child towards the Buddha, urging him to claim 'his heritage' – that is, to receive confirmation of his right to the throne (left, a 5th-century depiction of this event). But for the Buddha, who had renounced everything but the discovery of the Good Law, there was no other inheritance but his Teaching. Won over by his father, Rāhula followed him to the hermitage in the Banyan Grove, where he was ordained by the two primary disciples.

was contemplating and, simultaneously, from the throne.
He joined the Order and was ordained a week later, at
the same time as Rāhula, whose mother had ill-advisedly
sent him to claim 'his inheritance' from his father. It is
believed that during this sojourn a total of eighty
thousand Śākyas, 'one per family', were converted.

The gift of the Śrāvastī hermitage

On the way back to Rājagriha, six Śākya princes and
their barber, Upāli, joined the Order. Among the princes

were several of the Buddha's cousins, including
Ānanda, the Buddha's future attendant, and
Devadatta, the Buddha's jealous rival. All
were ordained at the same time.

During the brief stay in Rājagriha, a rich
merchant named Anāthapindāda visiting
from Śrāvastī converted after seeing and
hearing the Buddha. Anāthapindāda
urged the group to return with him to
his city. The Blessed One agreed, on
the condition that he and the
monks could live on the
outskirts of Śrāvastī
instead of within it.

Śrāvastī, the capital of
Kośala (an ancient Indian
kingdom in the region of

modern-day Nepal), was ruled by Prasenajit, King Śuddhodana's brother-in-law. He always honoured the Buddha and offered him unfailing friendship, even though his conversion has not been established with any certainty. Through the generosity of Anāthapindāda, Śrāvastī's first monastery, Jetavana ('grove [of Prince] Jeta'), was soon established. Considered the centre of learning, Jetavana would become the Buddha's favourite retreat and headquarters for the instruction of the monks. The Buddha's cell there, the Gandhakutī ('perfumed cell'), would be identified in the Commentary of Buddhaghosa as one of the Four Inalterable Sites (the three others being those of the Awakening,

Śrāvastī, capital of Kośala and one of the most important Indian cities in the Buddha's time, was not fortified until somewhat later (opposite, a photograph of its ruins). This was the spot where many of the major events in the Buddha's career took place. Jetavana Grove, on the city's outskirts – acquired by the merchant Anāthapindāda for an exorbitant quantity of gold – became the most important resting place for the Master and his Order. Centre and left above are a 19th-century Thai painting and a medallion sculpted on a pillar at Bhārhut in the 2nd century BC. Both illustrate Anāthapindāda's servants carrying in quantities of gold pieces to buy the grove. Texts speak at length about this lofty place of learning, of its consecration and the various structures that were built there. Custom in Buddhist regions requires that one uses the designation 'Jetavana' for the leading monasteries in the instruction of monks and the teaching of the faithful. Thus, in Angkor Wat, Cambodia, the famous Vishnu temple that in the 15th century became a leading Buddhist monastery for a long time also bore the name Jetavana.

of the Setting in Motion of the Wheel of the Law, and of the Descent from Heaven, in Sāṅkāśya).

Buddhism and women

In the fifth year following his Enlightenment, again in Vaiśalī, the Buddha was informed of the approaching death of King Śuddhodana. He immediately appeared before his father, 'flying through the air' to dispense to him one last teaching. (Buddhism always insists upon the importance of filial devotion. Parents are sacred, and their children should honour them even after their death. Family life is also extolled, and the obligation of husbands to their wives is given great importance.) King Śuddhodana thus died as the first layperson to have attained 'the state of perfection' (*arhattva*).

After her husband's death, Mahāprajāpatī, the aunt who had raised the Buddha, asked to be admitted into the Order. Her request first met with refusal, as traditional Brahmanism did not allow women admittance to renunciation and the Buddha did not wish to offend his contemporaries. The Buddha's cousin Ānanda had to intervene, reminding the Buddha of his aunt's past devotion to him. The Buddha gave in, and the Order henceforth allowed women to join. Still, they were bound to a stricter code than that of the men and were placed under the authority of the monks.

As the Buddha usually seems so painstaking in his duties towards his parents, one might be surprised at the coldness he displayed towards his aunt. But his opposition was only superficial and reflected the respect he had for the established order. His attitude towards women stemmed from a wish to respect Indian tradition,

If women were a threat to the male renunciants seeking salvation, it also happened, as evidenced by the plots against the Buddha, that they could be unlucky instruments in intrigues contrived by men (below, a temptress from a 5th-century cave painting from Ajantā). In the course of his

previous existences, the Bodhisattva was reborn several times as a woman.

Opposite: a scene from the Vessantara Jātaka.

which holds that women should live in a state of dependence on a male member of the family. Perhaps also his personal memories – particularly those of the assaults by Māra's daughters – made him fear the risks 'female magic' presented to the nascent Order.

The 'great magical wonder' of Śrāvastī

The sixth year following the Enlightenment, the Buddha found himself once again in Śrāvastī. There he encountered six teachers of rival doctrines, well known through other sources and confusingly labelled 'heretics'. They cannot have been indifferent to the Buddha's progress and no doubt did not show him loyalty. A confrontation appeared inevitable, and a public debate in the presence of King Prasenajit was anticipated. After the debate – though he had recently forbidden monks to make use of their magical powers to win converts, urging that they be used only out of compassion and wisdom – the Buddha performed a 'great magical wonder', a repetition, with some embellishment, of the performance he had given a few years earlier in Kapilavastu. Variously described in the texts, the marvel is often given the name 'miracle of the mango tree', either because a mango tree served as the setting or because one sprouted magically at the bidding of the Blessed

One. The Buddha first performed the 'twin miracles' (alternating productions of fire and water), then materialized and multiplied his own image in four positions: standing, walking, sitting and lying down. The confusion among those of contrary beliefs – no doubt hastened by the intervention of supernatural forces – was total. One of them, Pūrana, even drowned himself. The miracle of Śrāvastī belongs to the series of the Four Great Miracles, which is added to that of the Four Primordial Miracles (Final Birth, Attainment of Enlightenment, Setting in Motion of the Wheel of the Law and Total Extinction).

Sojourn in Indra's heaven

A visit to the heaven of Indra, premier among the thirty-three gods, was a duty of all Buddhas. It was there that the Blessed One went after performing the 'great magical wonder' at Śrāvastī to spend the three months of the rainy season teaching the 'pure and simple' Doctrine to his mother, who had been reborn among the gods without the benefit of such instruction. A great number of divinities gathered near the Buddha, who gave the Teaching seated on Indra's own throne.

The debate held in Śrāvastī and judged by King Prasenajit must have confounded the heads of rival sects hostile to the triumphs of the Buddha and his Teaching. The winner of this sort of public discussion, under any condition, enjoyed increased influence. This time, even though as a rule he rejected such things, the Buddha felt it necessary to win popular support through a demonstration of his supernatural powers. First he performed the 'twin miracles', consisting of making water jet from his feet and flames shoot forth from his shoulders (left). Then came the 'miracle of the mango tree' – in the tree's foliage, the Buddha manifested symmetrical images of himself in four postures – standing, walking, sitting and lying down. This Thai painting (opposite) dating from 1734 depicts only three of these postures.

While the ascension into Indra's heaven seems to have occurred without witnesses, the return took place in the presence of an immense crowd. At the end of the rainy season, before one of the gates of Sāṅkāśya, the Blessed One, accompanied by various gods, descended a staircase that had been specially constructed by the gods. As he placed his foot on the earth, the gathered assembly had a clear view of the entire spectrum of 'visible' worlds, from the third stage of the world of meditation of Brahmā to Avīci, the deepest hell. Despite its highly mythical nature, this miracle, one of the Eight Great Miracles, is the one that is related with the fewest variations among the texts.

The last sermons

For the Buddha's contemporaries, the return from Indra's heaven seems to have marked the moment when the Buddha, the Doctrine and the Saṅgha were enjoying the highest authority. It could not help but result in new difficulties, reflecting jealousy from various quarters.

Throughout the years of the Buddha's peregrinations, often marked more by vile acts than by clear progress of the community of the faithful, certain periods appear to be devoid of notable events. This occurs to such a degree that some authors have speculated about the true duration of the Buddha's Last Existence, thinking there might have been an intentional prolongation of some fifteen years to maintain the appearance of his having lived a full human life.

But the absence of facts is really not so surprising. The opportunities for resounding conversions are not infinite, not to mention those accompanied by miracles. As it would have been easy to invent a few fantastical anecdotes, one must believe – in agreement with the Orientalist Jean Filliozat – that the silence of the texts vouches for the integrity of their authors. Thus, only a few episodes

A 2nd-century BC bas-relief from Bhārhut (above left). Seated under the magical tree planted in front of the assembly of gods in Indra's heaven, the Buddha reveals the Good Law to his listeners.

are reported, two of which take their place among the greatest miracles. Others reveal the darkness of the designs on the part of rival sects.

Shortly after his return from Sāṅkāśya, the Buddha sojourned at Jetavana. Ciñcā, a female member of an itinerant sect, was pushed by her teachers to put the Buddha in a compromising position by claiming to have

The Descent from Heaven was a favourite subject on the Indochinese Peninsula. They delighted in extolling the Buddha's serenity and the fervent jubilation of the gods.

become pregnant by him. But she tried too hard to be convincing. Her cunning deed backfired, to her shame, and as she fled Jetavana under shouts and boos, the earth opened up beneath her and cast her into the deepest hell.

Later, again at Jetavana, an even more devious intrigue was contrived, this time using as its instrument Sundarī ('the beautiful'), whose mortal remains were purportedly found buried near the Buddha's cell. The plotters, however, did not succeed in implicating the Blessed One, and their crime was punished by human justice.

The miracle of Pārileyyaka Forest

In the seventh year after the Enlightenment, two conversions show how the Law applies to everyone and how great is its power, even over the most vile of beings. First was that of Yaksha Ālavaka, an ogre of immense

The Buddha's retreat in the Pārileyyaka Forest near Kauśāmbī (to the southwest of modern Allahābād) occupies an important place in southeast Asian beliefs (opposite left). The miraculous assistance and veneration of the Buddha by a lone elephant and a monkey yielded to these two beings born in an 'unfortunate condition' (because they were incapable of discerning good and evil) almost immediate rebirth in the realm of Indra, who showed them the way to salvation.

That a child, having nothing else to offer the Buddha begging his daily food, makes a gift of a fistful of dust might seem ridiculous, if not shocking. Fifth-century sculptors in Ajantā nonetheless found the scene instructive (opposite right). In Buddhism, an intention is always more important than its consequences, which are often dependent on chance.

Buddhist hells are akin to Christian purgatories where beings, before being reborn, receive immediate retribution for sins committed through conscious violation of moral precepts. Depictions of these hells, such as this one (left) from Bangkok, promote moral vigilance.

powers who terrorized an entire city, and then, four years later, that of the bandit Aṅgulimāla ('garland of [cut-off] fingers'), the delinquent son of a brāhman who had entered into the service of an evil master.

During the tenth year, the Buddha is said to have retired alone into the Pārileyyaka Forest, where he enjoyed the company and devoted assistance of a lone elephant and a monkey. This marvel enjoys tremendous popularity because it shows the value of retreating on one's own to the forest and the good that comes for all beings of contact with the Buddha.

Devadatta's transgressions

In the thirty-seventh year following the Enlightenment,

around the time of the death of King Bimbisāra, Devadatta thought he might finally be able to rid himself of the Buddha, his cousin, of whom he had been jealous through so many existences and whom he now hated. First he tried to install himself as head of the Order, citing 'the advanced age' of the Buddha, who, knowing full well the thoughts of all beings, would never have consented to this. Next he decided to turn to a more expeditious method – murder by hired assassins. Powerfully affected by the sight of the Blessed One, the assassins became converts. Another attempt, a staged accident involving a rock being rolled down the slopes of Vulture Peak Mountain (Gridhrakūta) as the Buddha passed by, caused him only a minor wound.

A Tibetan artist created this convincing portrayal of the elephant Nālāgiri being tamed by lions springing forth from the Buddha's fingers (above). Yet it does not show the power of the Buddha's benevolence, so evident in the relief from Amarāvatī (opposite above), which contrasts the terror provoked by the 'man-killing' elephant with his gentle submission to the Buddha.

Frustrated by the collapse of his plans, Devadatta called upon the irrational fury of an animal. His choice fell on Nālāgiri, an elephant trained for warfare. First intoxicated to arouse his anger, the beast was set free to run wild along the streets of Rājagṛiha during the time of the daily begging. Panic broke out among the people, but the Buddha remained unperturbed, and Nālāgiri, moved by his benevolence (*maitri*), knelt at his feet and was instantly cured of his murderous insanity. Another one of the Eight Great Miracles, Nālāgiri's submission also enjoys particular renown.

Despite all his failed attempts on the Buddha's life, Devadatta did not give up. In fact, it is he who is blamed for the creation of a schism in the Buddhist religion, traces of which were still evident when the Chinese pilgrims visited India in the 3rd to 8th centuries AD. Devadatta eventually died, after a long and difficult sickness, and was reborn in 'Avicī hell'.

Perhaps concerned more with artistic presentation than with spirituality, artists of Gandhāra (in present-day north Pakistan and part of Afghanistan) were attracted to the story of the Buddha's encounter with Devadatta's hired assassins. Though one might regret the presence of a bodyguard next to the Buddha, it is manifestly to his personal power that murderous intentions yield (below).

G.12
AR3280

The Buddha had come to the last year of his final existence. Knowing death was near, he continued to devote himself to the Teaching and to providing counsel to various parties – in particular, the Order, which would soon be deprived of its leader: 'Here I am, having become a weak old man; I am at the end of the road.... You must turn to yourselves. Have no other guiding light but the Law, no other refuge but the Law.'

CHAPTER 5

ATTAINING MAHĀPARINIRVĀNA

Under a canopy of sal trees that had spontaneously blossomed, the Buddha stretched out 'in full consciousness' in the presence of disciples and gods (right and detail opposite, a Sri Lankan mural). His body was surrounded by a halo of five colours: orange, white, red, yellow and blue. Much later, these colours would constitute the Buddhist flag.

Shortly before his death, the Buddha visited the city of Vaiśālī, where a meal was offered him by the courtesan Āmrapālī (right). In accepting her invitation, he had to turn down one from the governing princes of the city, thus emphasizing, once again, that the merit of an action does not depend upon the social position of the giver. Later, converted by a sermon given by her son who had become an eminent monk, Āmrapālī joined the Order and attained the status of arhant.

The last journeys

A tireless servant of the Law, the Buddha hastened the pace of his journeys despite his declining strength. Leaving Rājagriha with a sizable group of monks, he undertook a visit to Pāṭaliputra (present-day Patna, in northeastern India) and extolled the benefits of morality to the inhabitants of the city.

The Buddha and Ānanda then went alone to Bamboo Village (Venugrama) for the rainy season retreat. By now gravely ill, the Buddha could no longer ignore the imminence of his end and revealed to Ānanda that the Order should henceforth only rely on the Law.

Around this time, the Buddha's two greatest disciples, Śāriputra and Maudgalyāyana, died – the first during a visit to his mother, the second two weeks later, in an ambush attributed to one of the factions of detractors. It is claimed that Maudgalyāyana found the strength to drag himself all the way to the Buddha in order to expire at his feet, in this way ensuring his entry into nirvāṇa.

'And the earth shook'

During the passage to Cāpālacaitya, a venerated spot in Vaiśālī, the Blessed One might have suggested that Ānanda ask him to extend his existence 'until the end of

the cosmic era'. But Ānanda, perhaps in meditation, did not seize the opportunity in time, and Māra took advantage of the moment to remind the Master of his promise to 'enter into nirvāṇa once the Order was established and instructed'. In the same instant, 'in full consciousness and knowledge, the Blessed One rejected "his vital constituents" and soon after the earth shook....' Ānanda wondered what had caused this and, once he understood what had happened, worried that he would be blamed for his lack of attention or intuition.

The Buddha then came before the monks who had gathered in Vaiśālī and urged them to practise the Doctrine that they had been taught so that the faith would survive a long time. At the end of the rainy season, the Buddha recommended his journey through various villages in northeastern India.

Cunda's meal

Arriving in Pāpā, the Buddha and his companions made a stop at a mango plantation. There, the owner, a blacksmith named Cunda, invited them to take their daily meal with him. He served the travellers several succulent dishes, including a 'pork treat', which seemed to worsen the illness from which the Master suffered. (Although a number of writers have thought it necessary to explore the actual nature of this 'treat', which unquestionably triggered an event both awaited and feared by the Order, one must remember that the Buddha exonerated Cunda of all responsibility and even insisted on the highly meritorious nature of his gift.) Despite the worsening of his condition, the Buddha made ready to leave again, desirous of reaching Kuśinagara (present-day Kasia, in Uttar Pradesh), set as the goal of his final voyage, as quickly as possible.

From Pāpā to Kuśinagara

The last stretch, a distance thought to be about thirty kilometres, was covered only by much painful effort. When they were about halfway, the Buddha sat down at the foot of a tree. As he wished to quench his thirst, he asked Ānanda to fetch some water from a nearby stream known as the Kakushthā. The water had been muddied by the recent passage of a long convoy of carriages, but, because of the power of the Blessed One, it

A Thai artist has illustrated the episode of the 'pork treat' Cunda offered to the Buddha by referring to the local method of preparation: a suckling pig spit-roasted (left). But the artist underscores the importance of the event through the presence of a musician-god and even of the god Indra, recognizable because of his dark complexion.

instantly regained its clarity.

A moment later there arrived a Malla prince, Putkasa, a disciple of one of Gautama's first teachers. He had been travelling to Pāpā, but he halted upon seeing the Buddha. The prince received instruction from the Blessed One, was converted and gave the Buddha an offering of two garments made of gold-coloured cloth. After he left, Ānanda noticed that the garments seemed to lose their brilliance when placed against the Blessed One's body. Dumbfounded, he asked the reason for this marvel and was told that such things happen on two occasions: the eve of the attainment of Enlightenment by a Bodhisattva and the eve of the Total Extinction of a Buddha. A little further down the stream, the Buddha took a bath that revived his strength a bit and helped him to continue a small distance along the road. Yet bouts of weakness forced him to stop in a number of locations (certain texts mention twenty-five) before reaching another river, the Hiranyavatī. Crossing it, the travellers entered Kuśinagara, capital of the region governed by the Mallas. The tiny band headed southwest, towards Upavartana, finally stopping in a grove of sal trees.

The Buddha's sojourn near the stream Kakushthā is illustrated as if it were taking place in Thailand at the beginning of the 19th century (left), providing an excellent documentation of daily life in rural Thailand.

Ānanda respectfully presents the Buddha with the water that he has fetched for him (below).

'All component things are perishable'

As soon as he arrived, the Buddha had Ānanda prepare a bed between two sal trees. He wanted to lie 'in full consciousness' on his right side, stretched out with his head towards the north, facing west, a position from which he would never rise again. He spent the first two watches of the night instructing and comforting people.

To Ānanda, unable to control his grief and upset at the choice of such an undistinguished spot for such an important event, the Buddha explained that, on the contrary, this city, to which he had come before and in which so many followers of the Doctrine lived, had also been his capital in ancient times, when he had been a Universal Monarch. (To emphasize this, some texts add that it was there in the sal tree grove that Buddha Pushya, the Buddha Gautama's seventh predecessor, 'had attained nirvāṇa'.) The Buddha, grateful for Ānanda's devotion and wishing to console him, promised that he would obtain the status of an arhant.

The Mallas, told of the imminence of the Blessed One's end, arrived in droves to pay him homage. Among them was the ascetic Subhadra, whom Ānanda tried to dissuade from visiting his Master, who was 'so tired'. The Buddha nonetheless gave him an audience, allayed his doubts and converted him, granting him immediate ordination.

Again going over several points of discipline important to the Order, the Buddha urged the monks who were present to ask as many questions as they wished concerning the Doctrine or the Discipline. To Ānanda's surprise, everyone kept quiet. Finally, the Buddha uttered

Not all images of the reclining Buddha depict Mahāparinirvāṇa. The stylized trees in this early 19th-century lacquer painting (opposite above) allow one to identify this episode as the Buddha's stop in the mango grove. During his final retreat outside Vaiśālī, the Buddha, already very ill, gives his final instructions (opposite below).

Informed by Ānanda of the Buddha's impending death, the Mallas of Kuśinagara hasten to see him. This work provides valuable documentation of Thai funeral rites at the beginning of the 19th century.

these words – his last – to the assembled audience: 'All component things are perishable; work diligently on your own salvation.'

Mahāparinirvāṇa

During the night's last watch, the Buddha completed an entire cycle of meditations, which led him by stages to the 'domain of the cessation of consciousness and feeling'. Immediately thereafter, he died. Thus, on his eightieth birthday (according to Pāli tradition), the fourth great miracle was accomplished. And, just as with the Final Birth, the Enlightenment and the Setting

in Motion of the Wheel of the Law, the earth shook, gods appeared and trees spontaneously burst into bloom.

Among the vast crowd that had gathered, those who had attained arhantship manifested only a state of peaceful contemplation, but those who were still 'on the way' could not contain their grief. 'Too soon has the Blessed One died, too soon has the One Who Has Attained the Realm of Bliss (*sugata*) expired. Too soon has the "eye of the world" closed.'

Even though the major disciples and those who had reached the status of arhant had already attained nirvāṇa when the Buddha's death occurred, his attainment of Mahāparinirvāṇa was a completion. (Etymologically, *nirvāṇa* means 'extinction', but it also signifies calm, peace. A state without a beginning, unchanging, inalterable, imperishable, it is not annihilation, but a nonbirth, a nonbecoming. Unattainable except through the extinction of the Self, it is an eternal, nonlocalized state. Beyond logic or rationality, it cannot be imagined; words are incapable of describing it.)

The funeral

The funeral rites – performed not by the Order but by laypeople – were orchestrated by the Mallas with spectacular display. For seven days,

This large standing statue (opposite) is part of an ensemble in Sri Lanka that also includes two seated images of the Buddha – one inside a cave, the other out-of-doors – and is completed by the colossal image of the Buddha reclining (left). For a long time, the standing figure was identified as Ānanda, until it was observed that on his head was an *ushnīsha*, a cranial protuberance strictly and uniquely characteristic of the Buddha. Furthermore, a standing position would not be very respectful on Ānanda's part. The image, by its posture, could only represent the Buddha contemplating the Bodhi Tree. All of these statues once were roughly sheltered with lightweight materials of which only traces now remain.

An image depicting Mahāparinirvāṇa, this reclining Buddha (opposite) is the subject of an illumination in an early 12th-century palm-leaf manuscript from Bihar. Below the reclining Buddha, one can see monks demonstrating their grief.

Reduced to their essentials, the facts relating to the Buddha's funeral are exalted in this Tibetan painting (left) by an ascending composition dominated by a stūpa, asserting the triumph signified by the Total Extinction of the Blessed One.

●Mahākāśyapa possesses a great, prodigious power that he has been given by the four supernatural powers. Thus, when he uttered the required stanzas, the Buddha's funeral pyre burst into flames by itself without anyone setting fire to it. "Now a raging fire burns whose flames are so intense it is impossible to stop it. Through this incineration, without a doubt the body will be entirely burned." The goddess of the sal trees was then beside the Buddha's funeral pyre. Having a sincere belief in the Buddha's Path, she was able to suddenly extinguish it using her supernatural forces. The Mallas then said among themselves: "Let us all collect the perfumed flowers that are found on all sides within twenty leagues of Kuśinagara, bring them and make of them an offering to the Buddha's body." ●

André Bareau
En suivant Bouddha
1985

musical processions, dances, and offerings of flowers and perfumes followed one upon the other. Washed and swathed in numerous shrouds, the Blessed One's body was bathed in oil, and placed in a metal coffin to be carried to the cremation site.

A number of writers have been surprised at how these arrangements resemble the funeral rites of rulers with claims to universal sovereignty. (Several modern texts contend that what was surprising was that the Buddha himself asked for them.) But such statements are made with disregard for the fact that the Buddha always sought to be a 'servant' of the Dharma, the Law that he had discovered and which he wanted to spread throughout the world. In the context of the age, this was indeed the duty of a sovereign. It is stated in the stanzas to Śaila, and the *Lalitavistara* confirms it: 'One who holds absolute superiority over all the laws...the victor [*jina*], lord of the law...after having set in motion the Wheel of the Law, is called the King of the Law.'

The procession carried the body to the cremation site. At first the pyre could not be lit. Someone observed that

Visiting Kuśinagara (above) at the beginning of the 7th century, the Chinese pilgrim Hsüan-tsang counted nine stūpas there. Some commemorated the Buddha's previous lives, others were of Mahāyāna inspiration. One was erected after the attainment of nirvāṇa by Subhadra, the last monk to be ordained by the Blessed One. On the spot where the funeral pyre spontaneously burst into flames, a stūpa was erected by Aśoka. A recently discovered copper plate comes from the stūpa built on the death site.

A late-19th-century painting from northern Thailand (left) effectively evokes the contrast between the suffering the Buddha's death caused the monks still in pursuit of liberation and the serenity of those who had already attained arhant status.

the duty of lighting the fire belonged to the primary disciple, Mahākāśyapa, 'the eldest son'. Previously unable to join the Master but now informed of his death by a sort of miracle, he hastened to 'arrive at the feet of the Blessed One'. At the instant he appeared, the Buddha's feet burst from their wrappings as if to grant his wish. At the same time, the pyre spontaneously burst into flame. It later extinguished itself in an equally supernatural manner.

Partition of the relics

At the end of the ceremony, the bones were collected and carried off by the

The expansion of the cult of the Buddha's relics, whether corporal, material or commemorative, led to the making of stūpa-reliquaries, often portable (such as this Tibetan one, left), that re-created on a reduced scale the architectural features of actual stūpas erected in various regions.

Mallas, who wanted to keep them, as the death and cremation had taken place in their city. But various neighbouring princes also laid claim to them. War loomed. The brāhman Droṇa arbitrated the argument, suggesting the division of the relics into eight parts, keeping for himself the vessel utilized for the partitioning as an honorarium. Late arrivals, Mauryans or a brāhman, took the coals from the pyre. Each group, in accordance with the wishes of the Buddha himself, erected a stūpa over the relics they received. Legends sometimes add that human beings received only a third of the relics, while the gods and the Nāgas divided the remainder. Whatever the case may be, 230 years later, the relics belonging to humans were said to have been separated into 84,000 parts by 'Universal Monarch' Aśoka when he attempted to spread the Doctrine to the furthest reaches of his empire.

On various grounds, the Magadha king and the heads of the six neighbouring clans of Kuśinagara demanded from the Mallas a portion of the relics. The Mallas, however, felt they should be allowed to keep the relics, as the Buddha's cremation had taken place on their territory. Polite requests quickly became demands with weapons. The sculpted relief above (from a Sāñchī stūpa) depicts what nearly became the War of the Relics.

'O, monks, start then on your way, and go for the good of the many, for the happiness of the many, out of compassion for the world.… Preach the Law.… Preach it in its spirit and its letter. Show in the fullness of its purity the practice of the religious life.'

Divyāvadāna
('The Divine Exploits', presumed
to have been composed shortly
after the beginning of the Christian era)

CHAPTER 6

ADVANCING THE TEACHING

A Buddhist monk leaves an offering of flowers at the feet of a colossal (nearly twelve metres high) statue of the Buddha sculpted around the 9th century in Sri Lanka (opposite). This Nepalese manuscript in Sanskrit dating from 1184 (right), with its stylized writing against a black background, is a Mahāyāna text of Tantric inspiration dedicated to Vasudhārā, goddess of abundance.

After the Buddha's death, there was clearly no question of trying to find a successor. For the moment, the Good Law survived, and it was the responsibility of the Order to advance it, both by teaching and by example. The Blessed One had made it a rule to apply unceasingly the principles of the Law. He had never desired to impose himself as a leader but was content to give advice that might prove useful, especially to those members of the Order who led an itinerant life and thus had to face the harsh realities of daily life and the judgment of others.

Transmission of the Teaching

Because it had grown so rapidly, the Order was hardly monolithic but instead consisted of an ensemble of groups of varying sizes, all sharing the same faith but each one influenced by local cultures, with no specific plan and certainly no formal dogma.

With the Master gone, each group felt even more alone, as at first there was no written record of the Blessed One's words. It was unlikely that any one person had ever heard them in their entirety. Thus, there seemed to be a dual necessity: first, to preserve the Teaching, in words and in acts, of the Master and, second, to integrate and codify the disciplinary rules of the Order in order to stem schismatic impulses and suppress the quarrels that had begun to appear even during the Buddha's lifetime. While the need for this was felt by the majority, the problem remained to find someone with the

By dividing the relics into eight lots, the brāhman Droṇa rescued Kuśinagara from the War of the Relics. This 19th-century Thai depiction of the event (opposite), suggests a peaceful atmosphere. Note that the principal role falls to a brāhman but that Indra himself is also present, in flight, ready to receive a portion of the Buddha's relics to place in his heaven's reliquary.

Ānanda, who is standing, cannot control his grief (below). His posture, marked by a restraint inspired by the hand movements of Thai theatre, reveals not only his attachment to the Master but also his inability to overcome his emotions, having not yet reached arhantship.

requisite authority to undertake this important job.

Two of the leading disciples had already attained nirvāṇa. There remained Ānanda, singled out by the Buddha from the moment of his conversion and for more than twenty-five years his constant companion. As the person closest to the Buddha – and no doubt his most faithful witness – he was probably the most capable of heading the shaken community. But Ānanda, who had always been more preoccupied with the Blessed One and with others than with himself, had not yet attained

The disciples pay homage to the urn containing the body of the Blessed One (left). There is no sign of unhappiness; the general feeling is one of smiling serenity. This is a demonstration of a total 'cessation of suffering', the goal that each one has been seeking. According to this point of view, those who 'have a liberated spirit' cannot experience sadness.

arhantship. Having practised benevolence (*maitrī*) to a greater degree than that so easily egocentric vigilance (*apramāda*) that would have led him to the status of arhant long ago, he found himself excluded from the First Council when, at Mahākāśyapa's instigation, five hundred monks were called together to determine the future of the Order.

The time of councils

Convened during the rainy season following Mahāparinirvāṇa, the council – an assembly of high-ranking monks who came together to discuss questions of discipline and doctrine – was held at Rājagriha in the cave of Mount Vaihāra and lasted seven months. During the council session, Ānanda was accused of having

In the literature of Mahāyāna Buddhism, a particularly important place is held by the treatises dedicated to the Perfection of Wisdom (below). Thought to have originated in southern India, they were discovered preserved in the northern regions. Their length varies from 125,000 stanzas to only a few syllables. Dating from around 1145, the 8000-stanza treatise below is in the traditional format of palm-leaf manuscripts. The writing is read from front to back, lengthwise along each page; an illumination, more or less inspired by the content, occupies the middle portion.

The paintings of the Buddha's disciples in monasteries (left, a 19th-century Thai example) are intended to be lessons for the faithful as well as permanent examples for the Order.

The son of a brāhman, the disciple Mahākāśyapa (left) was an austere and strict man, qualities that prepared him for the role he would play in the Order at the time he convened the First Council.

Rājagṛiha ('king's residence') is reputed to have been visited by many legendary kings. At a nearby spot known as Vulture Peak Mountain (below), the Buddha is said to have given a sermon that constituted one of the bases of Mahāyāna Buddhism.

committed five faults (some texts say ten) while in the service of the Buddha. He withdrew in solitude and, within a few hours, reached arhanthood. Ānanda then rejoined the assembly and gave a full public confession, an act that would become a rule of the Saṅgha.

Questions related to points of Discipline (*vinaya*) were directed to Upāli, the former barber of the Śākyas. Ānanda's responses to questions about the Doctrine constituted the basis of the Texts (*sūtras*). These were not transcribed until shortly before the 1st century AD, but – as images reveal, of which the oldest date nearly two centuries

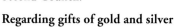

earlier – the essence of the 'Basket of Teachings' (Sūtrapitaka) had already been defined.

At the conclusion of the council, Mahākāśyapa, following the Buddha's model, continued his travels and teachings (certain of which are mentioned in the Pāli canonic texts), while Ānanda assumed leadership of the Order. Among the disciples that he instructed, Yaśas was the most important. Having been privileged to have known the Buddha, he would be called upon, when he was very old, to play an important role in the Second Council.

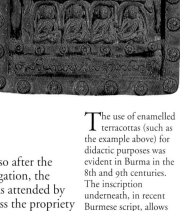

The use of enamelled terracottas (such as the example above) for didactic purposes was evident in Burma in the 8th and 9th centuries. The inscription underneath, in recent Burmese script, allows one to identify that it is the Third Council, in Pātaliputra, that is shown in this diagrammatic depiction.

Regarding gifts of gold and silver

Presumably convened a hundred years or so after the Buddha's Mahāparinirvāṇa, at Yaśas' instigation, the Council of Vaiśālī, or Second Council, was attended by seven hundred monks. Its goal was to assess the propriety of ten practices that had been adopted by the Vaiśālī monks, in particular, that of accepting gifts of gold or silver from adherents.

Yaśas, condemning these practices as contrary to disciplinary rules, found himself rejected by the Vaiśālians. The council then had to gather the Vaiśālī monks with monks of other regions who observed more traditional practices, including those living in more distant

areas recently won over to the Good Law (such as the kingdom of Avanti and the Deccan Plateau). A panel of eight judges, divided equally between Vaiśālians and Yaśas sympathizers, announced a verdict that ultimately led to the condemnation of the Vaiśālian practices, a verdict based on the prescriptions of the Pratimoksha, a noncanonical account of the very foundations of the discipline.

A doctrine for laypeople

The role of the monks and the historical importance of the councils should not obscure the fact that the Doctrine addresses itself above all to the lay community, without distinction as to place of origin or social status. From the beginning of its formation, the Order was composed of the Saṅgha – that is, the monks (*bhikshu*) – and the larger group of lay disciples (*upāsaka*). If the former devote their lives to spiritual development and to teaching the Dharma, or Law, the latter play no less an important role in their relationships with both family and society.

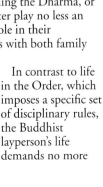

In contrast to life in the Order, which imposes a specific set of disciplinary rules, the Buddhist layperson's life demands no more

Not only richly decorative, the sculpture that adorns this pillar (left) is primarily a representation of the Buddha's person and his Teaching. It has been explained that the symbolism of this composition – which starts with the Buddha's footprints and ends with the Wheel of the Law surmounted by the Triple Jewel and graced with the royal parasol – is the very image of the Buddha's essence blended with his Teaching. More easily accessible than the later, humanistic images of the Buddha from the first centuries AD, such symbolic representations allow one to understand the emergence and rapid success of Mahāyāna Buddhism.

Transcriptions of Buddhist manuscripts – in Pāli or in Sanskrit – reflect local traditions. In Central Asia, a script inspired by that of Gupta India was used until the 7th century (opposite top). In Thailand, except in the north, and in Cambodia, Khmer *mūl* characters were used for Pāli texts (opposite bottom).

than a pledge, in the presence of a monk, to accept the Triple Refuge, sometimes called the Triple Jewels (the Buddha, the Law and the Saṅgha), and a vow to follow the Five Precepts that will guide one's moral conduct – one must not take another's life, steal, commit adultery, lie or consume intoxicants. If one follows the Five Precepts and

accepts the Triple Refuge, one is said to follow the Eightfold Path and may attain the saintly state of arhantship.

It should be recalled that in most forms of Buddhism, followers are not required to observe any rites or outward ceremony. Piety and tradition alone have led to the celebration of certain holidays or the veneration of relics and holy sites.

Aśoka and Buddhism

The twelfth successor to Buddha's friend King Bimbisāra, Aśoka the Mauryan (d. 238 or 232 BC), was converted six or nine years after his coronation, which itself occurred 218 years after the Mahāparinirvāṇa. During the eighteenth year of his reign, a Third Buddhist Council

The Wheel 'with a thousand spokes' (above left) symbolizes both the Buddha and the Law he taught. It also marks his feet and hands. The Buddha's footprint (or, rather, its imprint) tends to invoke a guarantee of protection of a given site by the Buddha and the Law.

was held in Pātaliputra, the new capital of Magadha, in response to the development of schismatic tendencies that had led Aśoka to issue three edicts against the instigators. But Aśoka's most remarkable effort, linked to the expansion of his empire to include all of Jambudvīpa (that is, the entire Indian subcontinent), was his ambition to spread the Buddhist religion as far and wide as possible.

As a result of the council, it was decided to send missionaries to nine regions. Among the territories, particularly notable (according to Pāli sources) are: Suvaṇṇabhūmi (which lay within the far reaches of present-day Thailand and lower Burma), Tambapanni (in modern Sri Lanka), Yonakarattha (the future Greek kingdoms of Sogdiana and Bactria) and the Himalayan regions. If it were still too early for the Suvaṇṇabhūmi mission to bear much fruit, the others, especially the mission to Sri Lanka led by Mahinda (who was either Aśoka's son or another close relative), played an essential role in the written conservation of the tradition.

Aśoka's benevolence remains legendary.

This Universal Monarch – *cakravartin*, 'one who possesses the Wheel' – displays the 'bodily marks of the great man'.

Auspicious signs, affirming the protection of the Blessed One, are very popular and increased after the 11th century, the ideal number being 108, a number considered the most eminent according to Indian theories.

An Indian woman (below) worships an image of the Buddha. Touching his feet is an act of individual piety corresponding to no specific prescription. Her act brings to mind ancient brāhmanic rites, as do the offerings of flowers or incense and the fabrics that occasionally drape the statues.

Buddhist monuments *par excellence*, reliquaries and commemorative structures venerated by the faithful, stūpas were not originally created by or for Buddhism. Their origins are intertwined with those of tumuli, which date back to the Bronze or Iron ages. In distant times, these monuments were massive constructions of brick or stone made of a base and a dome and surmounted by a pillar. At the beginning of the Christian era, their shape evolved into the conical form that now characterizes stūpas. The Ruvanveliseya Dagaba of Anurādhapura (left below), a Sinhalese stūpa restored in the 19th century, effectively re-creates the earlier shape. A stūpa in Bodhnāth, in Kathmandu (opposite above), is embellished with painted depictions of eyes and tufts of hair between the brows, a traditional attribute of Buddhas. Styles of stūpas are determined by the region. For example, in Ladakh, in northeastern Kashmir, the Tibetan form is dominant (opposite below). A 14th-century stūpa of Wat Mahathat, in Sukhothai, Thailand, is an elongated version of the primitive form (left above).

He was always mindful of Buddhist precepts, as his dealings with heretical sects (Ajīvika, in particular) show, despite the frequent hostility expressed for his beliefs, even among his kin. The most ancient known art honouring Buddhism is thought to have been made during his reign. If little remains of the stūpas he had erected on the sites of the great pilgrimages, some of the pillars that were built there are well known, such as the one he erected on the site of the First Sermon to commemorate his conversion. His legend, the *Aśokāvadāna* ('Aśoka's Exploits') was used throughout the centuries as a model for Buddhist sovereigns and Aśoka might be regarded as the most important lay follower, protector and propagator of the Triple Jewel: the Buddha, the Law and the Saṅgha, for the well-being of all.

The great stūpa of Sāñchi was built in the 2nd or 1st century BC on top of the remains of one constructed by Aśoka towards the end of his reign. The stone balustrade and four monumental portals were executed at the end of the 1st century BC. Its sculptures, gifts of pious donors, were crafted by woodcarvers, metalworkers and carvers of ivory. Conceived as a continuous narrative, the carvings depict numerous personages. They rarely illustrate the Jātakas, the principal themes of the ancient school (Bhārhut); scenes borrowed from the life of the Buddha and from the history of Buddhism are preferred. The pillars of the west portal (rear side, left) depict the First Sermon, symbolized by the Wheel. The three stūpas connote the partitioning of the relics. On the architraves are depicted the defeat of Māra, the attainment of Enlightenment under the Bodhi Tree, the War of the Relics and the siege of Kuśinagara.

In Sārnāth, to mark the spot where the First Sermon was given, Aśoka erected a monolithic, fifteen-metre-tall pillar. The lower part still stands at the site, while its capital (above) is now in the Sārnāth Museum.

The Chinese pilgrims who went to 'seek the Law in Western countries' beginning in the 3rd century AD (until Buddhism was proscribed by an emperor of the T'ang dynasty in 845) were classically represented in travellers' dress (left) and laden with works that they brought back to China for translation and dissemination.

The expansion of Buddhism

After Aśoka's reign, so crucial to the spread of Buddhism, a Brahmanic renaissance took place under the Śuṅga dynasty in the 2nd century BC. Although the object of several persecutions during this era, Buddhism did not slacken in its expansion into the central and western regions of India (as works of art found in Bhārhut and

Sāñchī bear witness). And numerous sects also prospered in the northwest (in regions under Greek rule) and southeast (Āndhra, Amarāvatī, etc.). It was towards the 1st century BC, with the invasions of the Śaka, Iranian nomads, that the expansion towards the oases of central Asia and the Far East began. Buddhism finally penetrated China in the 1st century AD.

The growth of Mahāyāna, the 'Greater Vehicle', asserted itself at the same time. The result of the schism first recognized at the Vaiśālī Council, its doctrine is based on speculation about the meaning of the Buddha's teachings. It is judged to be more elaborate than that 'of the ancients'. (Hīnayāna, the 'Lesser Vehicle'). Boasting a rich literature, it multiplies the number of Buddhas in space and time, exalts the career and role of the Bodhisattvas and downplays the importance of arhants. Its impact was considerable, even in regions traditionally associated with Theravāda Buddhism.

The Buddhist monastery Wat Phra Si Sanphet (below) was built in the 15th and 16th centuries in Ayutthaya, then the capital of Thailand, in the courtyard of the royal palace. Destroyed during the Burmese sacking of the capital in 1767, it was never restored.

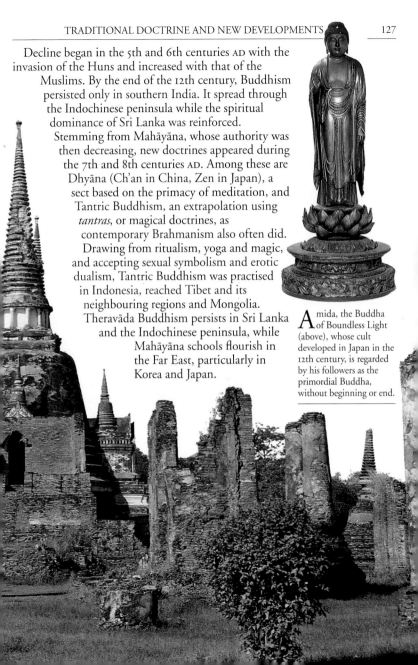

Decline began in the 5th and 6th centuries AD with the invasion of the Huns and increased with that of the Muslims. By the end of the 12th century, Buddhism persisted only in southern India. It spread through the Indochinese peninsula while the spiritual dominance of Sri Lanka was reinforced.

Stemming from Mahāyāna, whose authority was then decreasing, new doctrines appeared during the 7th and 8th centuries AD. Among these are Dhyāna (Ch'an in China, Zen in Japan), a sect based on the primacy of meditation, and Tantric Buddhism, an extrapolation using *tantras*, or magical doctrines, as contemporary Brahmanism also often did. Drawing from ritualism, yoga and magic, and accepting sexual symbolism and erotic dualism, Tantric Buddhism was practised in Indonesia, reached Tibet and its neighbouring regions and Mongolia. Theravāda Buddhism persists in Sri Lanka and the Indochinese peninsula, while Mahāyāna schools flourish in the Far East, particularly in Korea and Japan.

Amida, the Buddha of Boundless Light (above), whose cult developed in Japan in the 12th century, is regarded by his followers as the primordial Buddha, without beginning or end.

DOCUMENTS

From the Buddha
to Buddhism,
the birth of
a religion.

'Noble Truths', words of the Buddha

'Everywhere in the world where there are pleasant and delightful things, desire can dwindle and die.' A paradox? This is the Noble Truth of the extinction of suffering through the extinction of desire. The Buddha's Teaching places more emphasis on analysis, leading to knowledge, than on attempts to explain.

The First Sermon, or the Benares Sermon, is the explication of the Four Noble Truths that the Buddha discovered when he attained complete Enlightenment. These truths, which may seem fairly simple to those who are already familiar with them, were apparently difficult to grasp the first time, and the Blessed One was hesitant to teach a doctrine that an uninstructed listener might not comprehend. The delivery of this explanatory sermon is thus said to have marked the Setting in Motion of the Wheel of the Law, the beginning of the message that the Buddha would deliver again and again over the ensuing forty-five years until his Total Extinction and, thereafter, would be continued unceasingly by the Buddhist monastic community.

Setting in Motion of the Wheel of the Law

Monks, these two extremes should not be followed by one who has gone forth as a wanderer. What two?

Devotion to the pleasures of sense, a low practice of villagers, a practice unworthy, unprofitable, the way of the world (on the one hand); and (on the other) devotion to self-mortification, which is painful, unworthy and unprofitable.

By avoiding these two extremes the Tathagata has gained knowledge of that middle path which giveth vision, which giveth knowledge, which causeth calm, special knowledge, enlightenment, Nibbana [the Pāli word for nirvāṇa].

And what, monks, is that middle path which giveth vision… Nibbana?

Verily it is this Ariyan [noble] eightfold way, to wit: Right view, right aim, right speech, right action, right

The Wheel of the Law.

living, right effort, right mindfulness, right concentration. This, monks, is that middle path which giveth vision, which causeth calm, special knowledge, enlightenment, Nibbana.

Now this, monks, is the Ariyan truth about Ill:

Birth is Ill, decay is Ill, sickness is Ill, death is Ill: likewise sorrow and grief, woe, lamentation and despair. To be conjoined with things which we dislike: to be separated from things which we like, – that also is Ill. Not to get what one wants – that also is Ill. In a word, this body, this five-fold mass which is based on grasping – that is Ill.

Now this, monks, is the Ariyan truth about the arising of Ill:

It is that craving that leads back to birth, along with the lure and the lust that lingers longingly now here, now there: namely, the craving for sensual pleasure, the craving to be born again, the craving for existence to end. Such, monks, is the Ariyan truth about the arising of Ill.

And this, monks, is the Ariyan truth about the ceasing of Ill:

Verily it is the utter passionless cessation of, the giving up, the forsaking, the release from, the absence of longing for this craving.

Now this, monks, is the Ariyan truth about the practice that leads to the ceasing of Ill:

Verily it is this Ariyan eightfold way, to wit: Right views, right aim, right speech, right action, right living, right effort, right mindfulness, right concentration.

Monks, at the thought of this Ariyan truth of Ill, concerning things unlearnt before, there arose in me vision, insight, understanding: there arose in me wisdom, there arose in me light.

Monks, at the thought: This Ariyan truth about Ill is to be understood – concerning things unlearnt before, there arose in me vision, insight, understanding: there arose in me wisdom, there arose in me light.

Monks, at the thought: This Ariyan truth about Ill has been understood (by me) – concerning things unlearnt before, there arose in me vision, insight, understanding: there arose in me wisdom, there arose in me light.

Again, monks, at the thought of this Ariyan truth about the arising of Ill, concerning things unlearnt before, there arose in me vision, insight, understanding: there arose in me wisdom, there arose in me light.

At the thought: This arising of Ill is to be put away – concerning things unlearnt before…there arose in me light.

At the thought: This arising of Ill has been put away – concerning things unlearnt before…there arose in me light.

Again, monks, at the thought of this

The Buddha preaching the First Sermon.

Ariyan truth about the ceasing of Ill, concerning things unlearnt before… there arose in me light.

At the thought: This ceasing of Ill must be realised – concerning things unlearnt before…there arose in me light.

At the thought: This Ariyan truth about the ceasing of Ill has been realised – concerning things unlearnt before…there arose in me light.

Again, monks, at the thought of this Ariyan truth about the practice leading to the ceasing of Ill, concerning things unlearnt before…there arose in me light.

At the thought: This Ariyan truth about the practice leading to the ceasing of Ill must be cultivated – concerning things unlearnt before…there arose in me light.

At the thought: This Ariyan truth about the practice leading to the ceasing of Ill has been cultivated – concerning things unlearnt before there arose in me vision, insight, understanding: there arose in me wisdom, there arose in me light.

Now, monks, so long as my knowledge and insight of these thrice revolved twelvefold Ariyan truths, in their essential nature, was not quite purified – so long was I not sure that in this world there was one enlightenment with supreme enlightenment.

But, monks, so soon as my knowledge and insight of these thrice revolved twelvefold Ariyan truths, in their essential nature, was quite purified, then, monks, was I assured what it is to be enlightened with supreme enlightenment. Now knowledge and insight have arisen in me so that I know. Sure is my heart's release. This is my last birth. There is no more becoming for me.

'The First Sermon'
in *The Wisdom of Buddhism*
edited by Christmas Humphreys, 1987

Dhammapada: **words of truth (selected verses)**

The Dhammapada, *'verses on the Law' (*dhamma *is the Pāli word for the Sanskrit* dharma*), is one of the most celebrated Buddhist texts in the Pāli canon – celebrated as much for its literary value as for the edifying themes it addresses. Many of these verses belong to a common Indian heritage and can be found in Jain literature (Jainism is another religion that developed in India in the 6th century BC), as well as in classical texts.*

1. Mind foreruns (all evil) conditions, mind is chief, mind-made are they; if one speaks or acts with wicked mind, because of that, pain pursues him, even as the wheel follows the hoof of the draught-ox.

2. Mind foreruns (all good) conditions, mind is chief, mind-made are they; if one speaks or acts with pure mind, because of that, happiness follows him, even as the shadow that never leaves.

3. 'He abused me, he beat me, he defeated me, he robbed me,' the hatred of those who harbour such thoughts is not appeased.

4. 'He abused me, he beat me, he defeated me, he robbed me,' the hatred of those who do not harbour such thoughts is appeased.

5. Hatreds never cease by hatred in this world; by love alone they cease. This is an ancient law.

6. The others know not that in this quarrel we perish; those of them who realize it have their quarrels calmed thereby.

7. Whoever lives contemplating pleasant things, with senses unrestrained, in food immoderate,

indolent, inactive, him verily Māra overthrows, as wind a weak tree.

8. Whoever lives contemplating unpleasant things, with senses well-restrained, in food moderate, replete with confidence and sustained effort, him Māra overthrows not, as wind a rocky mountain.

9. Whoever, unstainless, without self-control and truthfulness, should don the yellow robe, is not worthy of it.

10. He who has vomited all impurities, in morals is well-established and endowed with self-control and truthfulness, is indeed worthy of the yellow robe.

11. In the unreal they imagine the real, in the real they see the unreal; they who feed on wrong thoughts never achieve the real.

12. Seeing the real as real, the unreal as unreal, they who feed on right thoughts achieve the real.

13. Even as rain penetrates an ill-thatched house, so does lust penetrate an undeveloped mind.

14. Even as rain does not penetrate a well-thatched house, so does lust not penetrate a well-developed mind....

21. Heedfulness is the path to the deathless; heedlessness is the path to death. The heedful do not die; the heedless are like unto the dead.

22. Distinctly understanding this difference, the wise in heedfulness rejoice in heedfulness, delighting in the realm of the Ariyas.

23. The constantly meditative, the ever earnestly striving ones, realize the bond-free, supreme Nibbāna.

24. The reputation of him who is energetic, mindful, pure in deed, considerate, self-controlled, right-living, and heedful steadily increases.

25. By sustained effort, earnestness, discipline, and self-control let the wise man make for himself an island which no flood overwhelms.

26. The ignorant, foolish folk indulge in heedlessness; the wise man guards earnestness as the greatest treasure.

27. Indulge not in heedlessness, have no intimacy with sensuous delights; for the earnest, meditative person obtains abundant bliss.

28. When the sagacious one discards heedlessness by heedfulness, this sorrowless wise one ascends the palace of wisdom and surveys the ignorant sorrowing folk as one standing on a mountain the groundlings....

76. Should one see a wise man, who, like a revealer of treasures, points out faults and reproves, let one associate with such a wise person; it will be better, not worse, for him who associates with such a one....

78. Associate not with evil friends, associate not with mean men; associate with good friends, associate with noble men.

79. He who imbibes the Dhamma abides in happiness with mind pacified; the wise man ever delights in the Dhamma revealed by the Ariyas.

80. Irrigators lead the waters; fletchers bend the shafts; carpenters bend the wood; the wise control themselves.

81. As a solid rock is not shaken by the wind, even so the wise are not ruffled by praise or blame.

82. Just as a lake, deep, clear, and still, even so on hearing the teachings the wise become exceedingly peaceful....

85. Few are there amongst men who go to the Further Shore; the rest of this mankind only run about on the bank.

86. But those who rightly act according to the teaching, which is well expounded, those are they who will reach the Further Shore (crossing) the realm of passions, so hard to cross....

90. For him who has completed the journey, for him who is sorrowless, for him who from everything is wholly free, for him who has destroyed all Ties, the fever (of passion) exists not....

94. He whose senses are subdued, like steeds well trained by a charioteer; he whose pride is destroyed and is free from the corruptions, such steadfast ones even the gods hold dear.

95. Like the earth, like an *indakhīla*, a balanced and well-conducted person is not resentful; like a pool unsullied by mud is he; to such a stable one life's wanderings are no more.

96. Calm is his mind, calm is his speech, calm is his action, who, rightly knowing, is wholly freed, perfectly peaceful, and equipoised....

98. Whether in village or in forest, in vale or on hill, wherever arahats dwell, delightful, indeed, is that spot.

99. Delightful are the forests where worldlings delight not; the passionless will rejoice therein, (for) they seek no sensual pleasures.

The Dhammapada
translated by Nārada Thera, 1954

Vasala Sutta: who is the pariah?

The text of the Vasala Sutta (sutta is Pāli for the Sanskrit sūtra, or Buddhist scripture) was delivered at Śrāvastī by the Buddha to a brāhman who had insulted him by treating him as an outcast or pariah (vasala).

1. Whoever is angry, harbours ill-will, is evil-minded and envious; whose views are delusive, who is deceitful, he is to be known as an outcast.

2. Whoever destroys life, whether bird or animal, insect or fish, has no compassion for life...

3. Whoever is destructive or aggressive in town and country and is a known vandal or thug...

4. Whoever steals what is considered to belong to others, whether it be situated in villages or the forest...

5. Whoever having contracted debts defaults when asked to pay, retorts, 'I am *not* indebted to you!'...

6. Whoever is desirous of stealing even a trifle and takes such a thing, having killed a man going along the road...

7. Whoever commits perjury either for his own benefit, for that of others or for the sake of profit...

8. Whoever has illicit affairs with the wives of his relatives or friends, either by force or through mutual consent...

9. Whoever does not support his father or mother, who are old and infirm, being himself in a prosperous position...

10. Whoever strikes or abuses by words either father, mother, brother, sister, or mother-in-law...

11. Whoever being asked for good advice teaches what is misleading or speaks in obscure terms...

12. Whoever having committed an offence

wishes to conceal it from others and is a hypocrite...

13. Whoever having gone to another's house and taken advantage of the hospitality there does not reciprocate in like manner...

14. Whoever deceives a priest, monk or any other spiritual preceptor...

15. Whoever abuses by words and does not serve a priest or monk coming for a meal...

16. Whoever, being enmeshed in ignorance, makes untrue predictions for paltry gain...

17. Whoever exalts himself and despises others, smug in his self-conceit...

18. Whoever is a provoker (of quarrels) or is avaricious, has malicious desires, is envious, shameless and has no qualms in committing evil...

19. Whoever insults the Buddha or his disciples, whether renounced ones or laymen...

20. Whoever not being an arahant pretends to be one, he is indeed the greatest rogue in the whole world, the lowest outcast of all. Thus have I exposed those who are outcasts.

21. One does not become an outcast by birth, one does not become a brahmin by birth. It is by deed that one becomes an outcast, it is by deed that one becomes a brahmin.

The Sutta-Nipāta
translated by H. Saddhatissa, 1985

The Buddha's essential teaching

A few months after hearing the First Sermon, a novice monk was quizzed on the doctrine he had been taught. In a single stanza, this novice conveyed so clearly the spirit of what he had learned that two men, Śāriputra and Maudgalyāyana, immediately converted. Śāriputra and Maudgalyāyana would later become two of the Buddha's chief disciples. Over the course of centuries, devotees have granted this particular verse such importance that it has been depicted on objects of worship, on the building stones of various structures and on relics preserved in stūpas. For Buddhists today it remains a ritual formula, repeated untiringly over and over again.

Of all Dharmas which have arisen from a cause, the Tathāgata has told the cause; and he has revealed its cessation, he, the great monk.

Translated by Etienne Lamotte

In Pāli:
Ye dhammā hetuppabhavā tesām hetum tathāgato āha/
Tesañ ca yo nirodho evamvādī mahāsamano//

In Sanskrit:
Ye dharmā hetuprabhavā hetum teshām tathāgato hy avadat/
Teshām ca yo nirodho evamvādī mahāśramanah/

Jean Filliozat
L'Inde classique, 1953

A Korean painting of the Buddha and his disciples.

Canonic texts

Soon after the Buddha's cremation, a council convened in Rājagriha to fix orally his words and his Teaching in Māghadī, a language similar to Pāli, spoken in the middle basin of the Ganges in those days. The most complete Pāli canon to have reached us was set in writing in the 1st century BC on Lāṅka (now Sri Lanka). It comprises three 'baskets': the Discipline (Vinaya), the Texts (Sutta) and a Summary of the Teaching (Abhidamma).

The Crocodile Jātaka

The Jātakas, or 'birth stories' (the Buddha's previous lives as well as those associated in diverse ways with his final existence), are tales, legends, or fables that show both the Bodhisattva's progress in his acquisition of virtues and how evil tendencies can persist from existence to existence. They belong to the 'Basket of Teachings' of the Pāli canon. The 'Crocodile' Jātaka, Sumsumāra Jātaka (number 208), tells of the tangles that the Bodhisattva, then born as a monkey, gets into with a crocodile, none other than the future Devadatta, and his wife, Ciñcā, the woman who would later attempt to compromise the Buddha at Jetavana.

Once upon a time, while Brahmadatta was king of Benares, the Bodhisatta came to life at the foot of Himalaya as a Monkey. He grew strong and sturdy, big of frame, well-to-do, and lived by a curve of the river Ganges in a forest haunt.

Now at that time there was a Crocodile dwelling in the Ganges. The Crocodile's mate saw the great frame of the monkey, and she conceived a longing for his heart to eat. So she said to her lord: 'Sir, I desire to eat the heart of that great king of the monkeys!'

'Good wife,' said the Crocodile, 'I live in the water and he lives on dry land: how can we catch him?'

'By hook or by crook,' she replied, 'caught he must be. If I don't get him, I shall die.'

'All right,' answered the Crocodile, consoling her, 'don't trouble yourself.

Detail of a Chinese manuscript of the Vinayapitaka.

I have a plan; I will give you his heart to eat.'

So when the Bodhisatta was sitting on the bank of the Ganges, after taking a drink of water, the Crocodile drew near, and said:

'Sir Monkey, why do you live on bad fruits in this old familiar place? On the other side of the Ganges there is no end to the mango trees, and labuja trees, with fruit sweet as honey! Is it not better to cross over and have all kinds of wild fruit to eat?'

'Lord Crocodile,' the Monkey made answer, 'deep and wide is the Ganges: how shall I get across?'

'If you will go, I will mount you on my back, and carry you over.'

The Monkey trusted him, and agreed. 'Come here, then,' said the other, 'up on my back with you!' and up the monkey climbed. But when the Crocodile had swum a little way, he plunged the Monkey under the water.

'Good friend, you are letting me sink!' cried the Monkey. 'What is that for?'

Said the Crocodile, 'You think I am carrying you out of pure good nature? Not a bit of it! My wife has a longing for your heart, and I want to give it [to] her to eat!'

'Friend,' said the Monkey, 'it is nice of you to tell me. Why, if our heart were inside us when we go jumping among the tree-tops, it would be all

A 2nd-century bas-relief illustrating the tale of the magnanimous monkey.

knocked to pieces!'

'Well, where do you keep it?' asked the other.

The Bodhisatta pointed out a fig-tree, with clusters of ripe fruit, standing not far off. 'See,' said he, 'there are our hearts hanging on yon fig-tree.'

'If you will show me your heart,' said the Crocodile, 'then I won't kill you.'

'Take me to the tree, then, and I will point it out to you hanging upon it.'

The Crocodile brought him to the place. The Monkey leapt off his back, and climbing up the fig-tree sat upon it. 'O silly Crocodile!' said he, 'you thought that there were creatures that kept their hearts in a tree-top! You are a fool and I have outwitted you! You may keep your fruit to yourself. Your body is great, but you have no sense.' And then to explain this idea he uttered the following stanzas: —

'Rose-apple, jack-fruit, mangoes too
    across the water there I see;
Enough of them, I want them not;
    my fig is good enough for me!

'Great is your body, verily, but how
    much smaller is your wit!
Now go your ways, Sir Crocodile,
    for I have had the best of it.'

The Crocodile, feeling as sad and miserable as if he had lost a thousand pieces of money, went back sorrowing to the place where he lived.

The Jātaka, or Stories of the Buddha's Former Births, edited by E. B. Cowell, 1969

The *Lalitavistara*

The Lalitavistara, *a Sanskrit canonic text, is a sūtra originally written in epic mode (the episodes reproduced here are taken from a later prose version) that narrates the life of the Buddha from his final existence among the gods in Tushita Heaven to the Setting in Motion of the Wheel of the Law. It is considered as an intermediary between the traditions of ancient and Mahāyāna Buddhism. The tendency to exaggerate the most minor facts should be viewed as attestation to the talents of the storyteller rather than any desire to take advantage of an audience eager for the marvellous.*

The birth of the Buddha

Now...Māyādevī proceeded forth attended by her suite. She was guarded by eighty-four thousand well-appointed horse-cars, eighty-four thousand well-appointed elephant-cars, eighty-four thousand brigades of heroic, veteran, sturdy soldiers clad in impenetrable mail and armour. She was preceded by sixty thousand Śakya maidens. She was guarded by forty thousand Śakyas, old, young and middle-aged, all born agnates to the king Śuddhodana. She was surrounded by sixty thousand musicians of king Śuddhodana's inner apartments, all engaged in singing and music, playing on clarions and other instruments. She was surrounded by eighty-four thousand Deva damsels, by the same number each of Nāga damsels, of

Grabbing the branch of a tree (above), Queen Māyādevī gives birth to the Bodhisattva through her right side (below).

Gandharva damsels, of Kinnara damsels, and of Asura damsels, proceeding in different arrays, decorated with a profusion of ornaments, and engaged in

singing, music, or pleasant conversation. The whole of the Lumbinī garden was redolent with scented waters, and besprinkled with choice flowers. All the trees in that noble park were clad with leaves, flowers and fruits out of season. That park was decorated by Devas, even as the Miśraka Park is adorned by them.

Now, Māyādevī, having entered the park and descended from her chariot, sauntered about in the company of human and heavenly damsels. Rambling from tree to tree, strolling from one parterre to another, now looking at this tree, then at another, she came near the waved-leaved fig tree (*Ficus infectoria,* Plaksha). It was the noblest of many noble trees, with well-disposed branches, bearing fine leaves and blossoms, covered with exquisite flowers, redolent of aroma, having clothes of various colours suspended from it, resplendent in the lustre of numerous jewels, having its root, trunk, branches and leaves set with all kinds of jewels, having well-disposed and far extending branches, standing on

ground even as the palm of the hand, covered with verdant green rivalling in colour the throat of the peacock, and soft to the touch like the down on the pod of the *Abrus precatorius.* About it dwelt the mothers of former Jinas, and around it resounded the music of Devas. It was auspicious, stainless, and pure. By the calm spirit of hundreds of thousands of Śuddhāvāsakāyika Devaputras, it was bent. It was bepraised by the bent heads of those who bore matted hair as their crown, (*i.e.,* hermits). This Plaksha tree did the lady approach.

Now, that Plaksha tree, feeling the glory of the Bodhisattva, lowered its head and saluted her. Now, Māyādevī, extending her right hand, resplendent as the lightning on the sky, held a branch of the Plaksha tree, and, looking playfully towards the sky, stood there yawning. At that time sixty hundreds of thousands of Apsarases, along with Kāmāvachara Devas, engaged themselves in her service.

Thus did the Bodhisattva remain thriving in the womb of his mother. And when ten full months had passed,

forth from the right side of his mother, he issued, with full memory, knowing everything, and undefiled by any uterine dirt, such as usually attaches to others.

The first seven steps
Immediately after his birth the Bodhisattva alighted on the earth; and at that time, piercing through the earth, a noble lotus appeared for the newly-born Bodhisattva Mahāsattva. The two Nāga kings, Nanda and Upananda, remaining in semi-developed form under the sky, bathed the Bodhisattva by pouring two streams of water, one hot and the other cold. Sakra [Indra], Brahmā, the guardians of regions, and the Devaputras by hundreds of thousands, who had come there, bathed the new-born Bodhisattva with scented water and well-blown flowers, and sprinkled the same about him. Two chāmaras [fly whisks], and a jewelled umbrella became manifest in the sky. The Bodhisattva, seated on the noble lotus, beheld the four quarters; he beheld it with the sight of a lion – with the sight of a Mahāpurusha.

At that time further birth being precluded by the maturation of the fruit of his former good works, the Bodhisattva obtained a transcendental sight, through which he beheld to the utmost the three thousand great thousand regions, along with all their towns, market towns, villages, provinces, kingdoms, and capitals, together with all the gods and human beings dwelling there. He perceived, too, the mind and habits of all created beings. Perceiving them, he looked to ascertain whether there was any person equal to him in good conduct, in meditation, in thorough knowledge, and in the exercise of all virtuous actions; but nowhere in the three thousand great thousand regions did he see any.

Now then, the Bodhisattva, dauntless and fearless as a lion, and unagitated, calling to mind and contemplating on the eight objects of reflection, and knowing the mind and habits of all beings, advanced seven steps towards the east, saying, 'I shall be the easternmost (foremost) in all virtuous actions, the source of all goodness.' While he advanced, the beautiful, white, wide-extended umbrella and the auspicious chāmaras, advanced along with him in the sky, and where he set his foot there sprouted forth lotuses. In this way he next advanced seven steps towards the south, saying, 'I shall be worthy of reward (*dakshinīya*) from gods and men.' Towards the west he advanced seven steps, and, stopping like a lion at the seventh step, with a cheering voice declared, 'I am the eldest on the earth; I am the noblest on the earth; this is my western (or last) birth; I shall bring to an end all birth decay, death and pain.' He advanced seven steps towards the north, and said, 'I shall be subsequenceless (without a north) among all creation.' He advanced seven steps downwards, and said, 'I shall destroy Māra and his army; I shall shower on hell the rain of the cloud of the great religion, and blow out the fire of the nether regions, so that they may be restored to happiness.' He advanced seven steps upwards, and, casting his look above, said, 'I shall be the observed of all who live above.' These were the words that were said by the Bodhisattva.

At that time the three thousand great thousand regions learnt well from this voice that this was the knowledge of things produced by the maturation of the works of the Bodhisattva.

The Lalitavistara, or Memoirs of the
Early Life of Śākya Siñha,
translated from the Sanskrit by
Rājendralāla Mitra, 1882

The Four Encounters

It may seem surprising that the Bodhisattva did not become aware of the misery of the human condition and of the serenity linked to the religious life until he was in his late twenties. But one should not overlook the degree to which idleness, luxury and pleasure can mask reality and deprive beings of sound judgment.

From his youth, the Bodhisattva intended to leave his family. His father feared that he would seek the path of deliverance and constantly surrounded him with the pleasures of the five senses. When he was fourteen, the Bodhisattva had his coach prepared for an outing and left by the eastern door of the city. By chance he saw an old man with white hair and a humped back, bent over a cane, walking with difficulty. He asked his coachman, 'Who is this man?'

'He's a dotard.'

'What is a dotard?'

'He has lived for many years, his faculties are dimming, his appearance has changed, his complexion is different. When he is seated, it is difficult for him to get up, he has little energy left. That's why he is called a dotard.'

'Will I escape the same fate?'

'Not yet.'

So the Bodhisattva made his team turn back and returned to the palace. Not yet free of the law of ageing, he became sad and could not experience pleasure. The king demanded of the coachman, 'Did the prince enjoy his outing?'

'He was unhappy.'

'Why?'

'He saw by chance an old man, that's why he's unhappy.'

The king feared that the soothsayers had told the truth and that the prince would soon leave his household. Immediately, he had the pleasures of the five senses increased.

A long time later, the Bodhisattva again ordered his coachman to prepare his coach to go for an outing and left by the southern gate of the city. By chance he saw a sick man whose body was thin and weak and who, leaning against a door, breathed with difficulty. He asked his coachman, 'Who is this man?'

'He is an invalid.'

'What is an invalid?'

'His four great elements have increased or diminished, he can no longer eat or drink, his breath is weak and thin, his energy is lessened by the impurities he has in him. That's why he is called an invalid.'

'Will I escape from this same fate?'

'Not yet.'

So, the Bodhisattva made his team turn back and returned to the palace. Thinking that he was not yet free of old age or sickness, he became sadder still. The king again demanded of the coachman, 'Did the prince enjoy his outing?'

'He is even unhappier.'

'Why?'

'By chance he saw a sick man, that's why he is unhappy.'

The king feared his son would soon leave the household, and had the daily and nightly pleasures of the five senses increased again.

A long time later, the Bodhisattva again ordered his coachman to prepare a coach to go for an outing, and he left by the western gate of the city. By

Leaving his palace, the Bodhisattva embarks on the life of an itinerant monk.

chance he saw a dead man who, carried by a few men, was followed by his grieving and wailing parents. He asked his coachman, 'Who is that man?'

'That's a corpse.'

'What is a corpse?'

'He has stopped breathing, his spirit has left him, he no longer has awareness of anything, he has left his village empty, he is forever separated from his parents. That's why he is called a corpse.'

'Will I escape this same fate?'

'Not yet.'

Thinking that he was not yet free of the laws of old age, sickness or death, he was sadder still. Immediately, the Bodhisattva had his team turn back to go home.

By chance he saw a man whose hair and beard had been shaved off, who wore the garb dictated by monastic law, who held a bowl in his hands and walked looking towards the ground. He asked his coachman, 'Who is this man?'

'He is an itinerant monk.'

'What is an itinerant monk?'

'He has self-mastery, he has a dignified manner, he always behaves with patience and compassion towards beings. That's why he is called an itinerant monk.'

When he had heard this, the Bodhisattva shouted three times, 'Very good!' Having thought about it, he became elated. Immediately, he got out of his coach and paid homage to the ascetic and asked him, 'Why are your appearance and clothes different from people living in the world?' [Receiving an explanation similar to that which the coachman had just given him,] once again, the Bodhisattva shouted three times, 'Very good!' Having reflected upon this, he became elated. He got back in his coach and returned towards the palace. By chance, there was a woman who, seeing the Bodhisattva, had thoughts of love for him and uttered this verse:

'Happy is the mother who has
   such a son!
Happy his father, too!
Happy is the wife who has such a
   spouse!
He will attain nirvāṇa!'

When he heard the word nirvāṇa, the Bodhisattva leapt with joy and thought, 'Will I myself attain supreme nirvāṇa?' On his reentry into the palace, he reflected on the fact that he was not yet free from the laws of birth, old age, sickness and death. The king demanded of the coachman, 'Did the prince enjoy his outing today?'

'At the beginning, he wasn't joyful, but by the time he came back, he was very happy.'

'Why was that?'

'During his outing, by chance he saw a dead man, that's why he wasn't joyful. On the way back, he saw an itinerant monk, that's why he became totally happy.'

The king again thought, 'The soothsayers spoke the truth; he will certainly leave this household.' So, he had the daily and nightly pleasures of the five senses increased again.

'Vinayapitaka of the Mahīśāsaka [School of Buddhism]'
in André Bareau
En suivant Bouddha, 1985

The practice of austerities

Also drawn from the Vinayapitaka ('the Basket of Discipline'), this version of the Bodhisattva's abandonment of austerities seems the closest to factual reality. There is no intervention by gods or by the Bodhisattva's mother, reborn among them.

There were then five men who followed the Bodhisattva thinking that, should he find the Way, he would preach the Doctrine to them. In Uruvilvā lived four women, Balā, Utpalā, Sundarā and Kumbhakārī, all of whom were attracted by the Bodhisattva's ideas and who said, 'If the Bodhisattva leaves his home to seek the Way, we will become his disciples. If he stays home to lead an ordinary lay life, we will become his wives or concubines.'

As soon as the Bodhisattva arrived in this village, he started to practise austerities and continued them for six years. Despite this, he was not able to see with his own eyes the supreme Doctrine of holy awareness. So he remembered, 'Long ago, when I was living with the king my father, one day I was sitting under a rose-apple tree and freed myself of thoughts of desire and other vile and pernicious things and

stayed immersed in the first stage of meditation, free of reasoning or reflection, filled with joy, happiness, and unified thought.' The Bodhisattva again had this thought, 'Following this way of meditation, can one truly exhaust the source of suffering?' And this answer immediately came into his mind, 'Yes, one can exhaust the well of suffering in this manner.' Immediately, using the strength of his energy, he cultivated and practised this awareness and, in proceeding in this way, he was actually able to exhaust the source of suffering. So the Bodhisattva thought again, 'Is it by means of desires and other vile things that one obtains this happiness?' And he recognized, 'No, it is not by means of desires and other vile things that one attains this happiness.' He again had this thought, 'Is it not by practising the absence of desire and by abandoning vile things that I obtain this happiness? It is certainly not by inflicting suffering on my body that I obtain it. At present, wouldn't it be better for me to eat a little boiled rice and a gruel of cooked grains to acquire sufficient strength?' Shortly afterwards, the Bodhisattva, finally abandoning the extremely severe fast that he had been engaged in until then, ate a little rice and a gruel of cooked grains in order to restore his forces sufficiently.

As soon as he had taken some food, the five men who were his followers were completely disappointed and left him, saying to one another, 'The ascetic Gautama is crazy, stupid, he has lost the Way. Does there not exist a Way of Truth?' And they departed on the spot.

'Vinayapitaka of the Dharmaguptaka [School of Buddhism]'
in André Bareau
En suivant Bouddha, 1985

Chinese pilgrims

From the 3rd century AD, Chinese Buddhists travelled west in search of 'the Good Law'. In 845, these pilgrimages were interrupted temporarily by Chinese emperor Wu-tsung's proscription against Buddhism, but they recommenced in 966 and continued until the middle of the 11th century.

Born into an educated family in Honan, an east-central Chinese province, Hsüan-tsang (602–64) joined a monastery at the age of twelve and was ordained as a Buddhist monk by the age of twenty. A leading scholar of both Hīnayāna and Mahāyāna schools, in 629 Hsüan-tsang travelled to India to gather the primary source materials he needed. He remained there for the next nineteen years, staying at the Nālandā monastery and returning to China with 657 sacred Buddhist works and numerous relics and images. Hsüan-tsang spent the remainder of his life translating Sanskrit texts into Chinese and recounting his travels in his Buddhist Records of the Western World.

Where Śākyamuni was born
The kingdom of Jie Bi Luo Fa Su Du [Kapilavastu, roughly 240 kilometres north of Benares; the Buddha Śākyamuni's birthplace] measures around four thousand *li* in circumference. There are ten deserted cities of unkempt appearance. The royal city is in ruins, and what its size was is no longer known. The palace that existed inside the capital measured from fourteen to fifteen *li* in circumference. It was constructed entirely in brick. Its ruins are still high and intact; it has been deserted for centuries. The villages are sparsely populated; there is no king at all, instead, every village has its own chief. The soil is rich and fertile, sowing and harvesting take place at regular dates; the seasons are never irregular. Formerly, there were around a thousand monasteries, whose ruins still exist.

Next to the palace a monastery can be seen, housing around thirty monks

A 7th-century portrait of the Chinese Buddhist scholar Hsüan-tsang.

from the Sammatīya school, allied to the Lesser Vehicle [Hīnayāna Buddhism]. There are two temples to gods; heretics occupy them indiscriminately.

Inside the palace, one can see the ancient foundations. It is there where the principal palace of King Śuddhodana [the Buddha's father] was located. On top of these foundations, a *vihāra* [residence of monks, also a place where they retired for meditation] was constructed, at the centre of which stood a statue of the king....

Nearby is a[nother] vihāra. It was at this spot where Śākyamuni entered his mother's womb. In the centre is a depiction of the Bodhisattva at the moment he descended to be reincarnated....

To the northeast of the spot where the Bodhisattva descended into his mother's womb, there is a stūpa. It was at this spot that the Rishi [or Seer] Asita cast the horoscope for this royal prince.

Soothsayers and auspicious omens
The day the Bodhisattva was born, a number of auspicious omens were observed. At that moment, King Śuddhodana called his soothsayers and told them, 'Here is a child who has just been born; what are his good and evil qualities? Collect your thoughts and respond clearly.'

'According to the predictions of the first saints,' they told him, 'and according to auspicious omens that shone at his birth, if he stays at home, he will be a holy king Cakravartin [Universal Monarch]; if he leaves his family and embraces the religious life, he shall attain complete Enlightenment.'

At the same moment, Asita appeared from a distant land. He knocked on the door and demanded an audience. The king was delighted; he went himself to greet him and offered him gifts, then invited him to sit on a throne ornamented with precious stones. He said, 'I didn't think that the great Rishi would deign to pay me a visit today.'

'I was quietly seated in the plain of the gods,' he responded, 'when all of a sudden I saw a multitude of gods leaping with joy.

' "From whence", I asked them, "come these transports of joy?"

' "Great Rishi," they answered, "you should know that on the island of Jambudvīpa, the first wife of King Śuddhodana, who is of the Śākya race, has given birth this very day to a royal prince who should attain complete Enlightenment and will possess great discretion." Having learned of this event, I ran to your residence to be able to see it; but one thing distresses me, I am old and decrepit, I will not be able to see the holy effects of his virtues.'

Devadatta and the elephant
At the southern gate of the city, there is a stūpa. It was at this spot that the royal prince engaged in games of strength with the Śākyas and threw an elephant into the air. The royal prince, through his abilities in the arts and numerous talents, won over all his fellows.

The son of the great king Śuddhodana, his heart filled with joy, prepared to return. His coachman was bringing him an elephant. As he was about to leave the city, Devadatta [the Bodhisattva's cousin], who was envious of his strength, arrived from outside and interrogated the coachman: 'Who is going to ride this so richly adorned elephant?'

'The royal prince,' he answered, 'is just about to return. That is why I am going to find him to bring him this elephant.'

Devadatta, transported by fury, took the elephant away, struck him on the brow and kicked him with blows to the chest. The elephant fell, obstructing the road in such a way that it was impossible to pass. As nobody was able to remove the beast, the crowd of people found themselves stopped. Sundarananda [according to another account, a colleague or relative of Devadatta], arriving some time later, asked who had killed this elephant.

'It was Devadatta,' he was told. So [Sundarananda] dragged the elephant out of the road. When he arrived, the royal prince asked who had committed this evil deed, killing this elephant.

He was told, 'It was Devadatta who killed it to obstruct the city gate. Sundarananda dragged it away and cleared the road.' So the royal prince lifted the elephant and, throwing it into the air, made it go beyond the city moats. At the spot where the elephant fell, the earth opened up and formed a deep chasm that has been called the 'elephant moat' ever since.

Site of nirvāṇa

In the kingdom of Ju Shi Na Jie Luo [Kuśinagara, where the Buddha attained nirvāṇa], the walls of the capital are in ruins, the villages offer only a dejected solitude. The brick foundations of the ancient capital occupy an area of around ten *li*. Inhabitants are few and widely dispersed, burgs and hamlets are deserted.

At the northwest corner of the city gates is a stūpa that was constructed by King Aśoka. There stands the ancient house belonging to Cunda. In the middle of this house is a well which was dug so that people could make offerings to the stūpa. Although it has been in use for

A view of Kuśinagara, the place where the Buddha attained nirvāṇa.

many months and years, the water is still pure and clear. Three or four *li* northwest of the capital is the river A Shi Duo Fa Di [Ajitavatī]. A short distance from the west bank is a forest of sal trees. This type of tree resembles the *hu* [oak], but its bark is a greenish white and its leaves smooth and bright....

The age's Honourable One, moved by great pity and submitting to the rules of life, judged it useful to enter into the world. When he had finished converting humankind, he immersed himself in the joys of nirvāṇa. Placing himself between two sal trees, he turned his head north and passed away. Then the spirits, armed with a diamond bludgeon, seeing the Buddha enter nirvāṇa, were overcome with grief and shouted at the top of their lungs: '*Ru lai* has left us; he has entered into the great nirvāṇa. We are left without a protector, without support. A poisoned arrow has pierced our breast and the flame of suffering burns and consumes us.'

The relics of *Ru lai* should naturally have homage paid to them; but it is in vain that you have made this difficult voyage; you will obtain nothing.'

Then the great kings asked for [the relics] with a humble voice. Finding themselves met with refusal, they reiterated their entreaties and said, 'Since our respectful requests have not been met, our powerful army is not far away.'

But the brāhman Rijūbhava spoke out to tell them, 'Think well; the age's Honourable One, endowed with a tender mercy, proved himself human and practised virtue; his renown resounded to the farthest *kalpa* [world age]; this I believe you all know. If today we turn to violence, it would be completely wrong. Now, here are the relics; they should be divided into eight parts in order that each of you may honour them. Why go so far as to use armed force?'

The Mallas obeyed his words and immediately set about dividing the relics into eight parts. But the master of the gods, Indra, spoke thus to the eight kings: 'The gods should also have their portion; be careful lest you abuse your power in arguing with them.'

Then the dragon kings, Anavatapta and Elāpattra, deliberated and said, 'Don't forget us in the sharing out. If you use force, despite your numbers, you will not be able to fight us.'

The brāhman Rijūbhava told them: 'Don't argue so loudly. You must give everyone an equal part of the relics.' Thus, he made three equal portions: one for the gods, the second for the crowd of dragons and he left the third part for humans.

in *L'Inde du Bouddha vue par des pèlerins chinois*, edited by Catherine Neuwese, 1968

With these words, they dropped their diamond bludgeon and fell to the ground, breathless with distress. A long time after, they picked themselves up and, hearts filled with sadness and love, spoke among themselves in this manner: 'To cross the vast ocean of life and death, who will serve us as boat and oars? To walk through the shadows of a long night, who will be from now on our lamp and flame?'

Disputes over the relics

After the Buddha entered nirvāṇa and his body was cremated, the rulers of the eight kingdoms arrived with four corps of soldiers. They sent the brāhman Rijūbhava to tell the Mallas, 'It was in this kingdom that humankind's guide passed away to nirvāṇa; this is why we have come from far away to ask for a portion of his remains.'

'The Tathāgata,' the Mallas answered, 'deigned to demean his greatness and to descend to this lowly land. He has passed away to nirvāṇa, the guiding light of the word! He is dead, the tender father of humankind!

The images of Buddhas

Thirty-two bodily marks distinguish both Universal Monarchs and Buddhas from ordinary beings. Yet only Buddhas wear monastic garb and execute gestures signifying either great moments in their career or aspects of their identity.

Physical characteristics of Buddhas

The 'thirty-two bodily marks of the great man' are testimony to merits accumulated during the course of prior existences. (The Buddha Gautama is thought to have recognized on his disciple Mahākāśyapa seven such markings.) Even today, in Tibet, bodily markings are used in the selection of the Dalai Lama's successor.

The bodies of Buddhas contain the thirty-two characteristics of the mahāpurisa. *The lists of these signs in the* Lalitavistara *and in the* Mahāvyutpatti, *while varying in particulars, essentially agree. Both differ from the Theravadin Buddhist description, which has a different order and numerous divergences in details. The latter list (*Mahāpadānasutta*) is reproduced here, accompanied by the corresponding terms given in the* Mahāvyutpatti *and their ranking in that list. The Buddha has:*

1. Well-planted feet, *suppatitthapāda* (30, *supratisthitapāda*);
2. Wheel marks on the base of the feet, *hetthā pādatalesu cakkāni* (29, *cakrānkitahastapāda*);
3. Projecting heels, *āyatapanhin* (31, *āyatapādapārshni*);
4. Long fingers, *dīghangulin* (28, *dīrghānguli*);
5. Soft, delicate hands and feet, *mudutalunahatthapāda* (26, *mrdutarunahastapāda*);
6. Hands and feet covered with a network of lines, *jālahatthapāda* (27, *jālāvanaddhahastapāda*);
7. Arched feet, *ussankhapāda* (25, *utsangapāda*);
8. Antelope limbs, *enijangha* (32, *aineyajangha*);
9. Hands that can reach to the

Bronze (left) and stucco (opposite) heads of the Buddha.

knees, with no bending, *thitako va anonamanto ubhohi pānitalehi jannukāni parimasati parimajjati* (18, *sthitānavanatapralambabāhutā,* 'arms hanging without bending standing upright');

10. Private member in a sheath, *kosohitavatthaguyha* (23, *koshopagatavastiguhya,* 'vesicular region and private member sheathed');

11 and 12. Golden complexion and delicate skin, *suvannavanna kāñcanasannibhataca* and *sukhumacchavin* (17, *sūkshmasuvarnacchavi*);

13. One hair for every pore, *ekekaloma* (21, *ekaikaromapradakshināvarta,* 'and leaning right');

14. Body hairs standing straight up, *uddhaggaloma* (22, *ūrdhvagaroma,* 'hairs reaching very high');

15. Upright limbs, like a brāhman, *brahmujjugatta*;

16. Seven protuberances (on the hands, feet, shoulders, branching of the trunk), *sattussada* (15, *saptotsada*);

17. The front part of the body like a lion, *sīhapubbaddhakāya* (19, *simhapūrvārdhakāya*);

18. Full shoulders, *citantaramsa* (16, *citāntarāmsha*);

19. The rotundity of a banyan tree, *nigrodhaparimandala* (20, *nyagrodhaparimandala*);

20. The branching of the trunk well-rounded, *samavattakkhandha* (14, *susamvritaskandha*);

21. Superior delicacy of taste, *rasaggasaggin* (10, *rasarasāgratā,* 'delicacy of taste for tastes');

22. A lion-jaw, *sīhahanu* (11, *simhahanu*);

23. Forty teeth, *cattālīsadanta* (6, *catvārimshaddanta*);

24. Even teeth, *samadanta* (7, *samadanta*);

25. Teeth without gaps, *aviraladanta* (8, *aviraladanta*);

26. Very white teeth, *susukkadanta* (9, *sushukladanta*);

27. Large tongue, *pahūtajivha* (12, *prabhūtatanujihva,* 'large and thin');

28. A Brahmā voice, *brahmassara* (13, *brahmasvara*);

29 and 30. Very dark eyes, *abhinīlanetta,* and ox-like lashes *gopakhuma* (5, *abhinīlanetragopakshma*);

31. A white tuft, *unnā,* between the eyebrows (4, *ūrnā*);

32. A protuberance on the crown of his head, *unhīsasīsa* (1, *ushnīshashirsha*).

Various traditions add to the thirty-two signs twenty-four 'supplementary marks' (*anuvyañjana, dpebyad bzan-po,* 'good harmonies'). These supplementary marks are for the most part less unique to the Buddha than are the preceding ones; many are traits of beauty common among ordinary people. This justifies the division of the physical characteristics of the Buddhas into two lists. The marks on the feet that are often found displayed on the footprint are also considered separately. They consist of a number of symbolic linear figures of good augur (wheel, swastika, etc.) and are mentioned only in the Theravādin tradition.

Jean Filliozat
L'Inde classique, 1953

The gestures of the Buddha

From its long prohibition against representing the Buddha in human form, a prohibition resulting in a delightful – and often strongly erudite – aniconic imagery, Buddhism seems to have inherited a keen sense of the holiness of images depicting the Blessed One. The sacred nature of representations, whether painted or sculpted, dictated a reverence among all sects for the large body of precise rules governing the portrayal, as well as the execution, of images of the Buddha.

In general, the image of the Buddha or Buddhas (the historical Buddha, past Buddhas and even the transcendent Buddhas belonging to the Mahāyāna tradition) is defined by a collection of original physical characteristics, a particular monastic garb lending itself to certain types of stylization and by more or less codified postures and gestures.

The bodily characteristics of a Buddha, evident from the time of his birth, are the marks (*lakshanas*) of the Great Man (not all of them expressible plastically), of the man eminent among all others, the Predestined One, as distinguished from ordinary beings, who is called upon, thanks to merits accumulated over the course of

innumerable prior existences (and which the *lakshanas* evidence), to become either a Universal Monarch or a Buddha. If, for artists, the manner of interpreting these marks varies depending on the era and the school,

W alking (opposite) or seated with legs hanging 'European style' (above), the Buddha's postures are very strictly codified.

form of apparitions during the 'great magical wonder' at Śrāvastī intended to confound the heterodox sects; they are the only ones deemed proper for monks: standing, walking, sitting and lying down. If the walking posture is depicted only rarely in sculpture (in Thailand, for example, in the Sukhothai school, using an idealized approach; or in Burma, in the Pagan school, in a more stylized manner) and if the supine position is reserved particularly, although not exclusively, for the depiction of the Total Extinction (Mahāparinirvāṇa), the seated and standing postures play a more important role. Furthermore, the latter is diversely represented: Indian style, with legs crossed in a variety of ways, or 'European' posture, with two legs hanging; only the posture said to be of renunciation, with one leg bent, the other hanging, so often used for Brahmanic divinities and often used for Bodhisattvas, is not acceptable for the Buddha. Associated with an ensemble of appropriate gestures that are more or less fixed, these postures allow the representation, or at least the evocation, of the majority of the salient events of the Buddha's life, at least starting with his renunciation of the worldly life (the Great Departure and the relinquishing of his princely adornments) and the quest for Enlightenment, up until the Mahāparinirvāṇa.

Thus, a choice of well-defined gestures must in principle in a painted or sculpted narrative scene – or even in an isolated image – allow identification of the most memorable moments in the Buddha's career....

If the list and the designation of the gestures (Sanskrit, *mudrās*) remain the

certain of them have taken on a true signifying value (the cranial protuberance, or *ushnīsha,* or hair with regular curls, for example)....

Postures and gestures are, in theory, inseparable, it being understood that a number of gestures can be accomplished only in a particular posture....

We will note here only the *four postures* in which a Buddha can be depicted. These are the ones in which the Buddha manifested himself, in the same, no matter what sectarian affiliation, we must nonetheless stress that Theravāda Buddhism (the so-called Lesser Vehicle, in opposition, and with a pejorative connotation, to Mahāyāna, the Greater Vehicle) ignored their definition and even the use of the term (Pali, *muddā*). We again observe that the role and function imparted to the mudrās differ profoundly depending on which particular hand gesture is used to evoke a more or less exact moment in the life of the historical Buddha or to characterize, in Mahāyāna Buddhism, one of the transcendent Buddhas.

The traditional list of mudrās

Of a much longer list describing Bodhisattvas and divinities of all ranks – as well as monks – six mudrās are retained for and considered as specific to Buddhas, a list that is strikingly limited, even if one refers to art documentation alone. In it, however, are two gestures that can be related without ambiguity to specific miracles. Here is the list included in all the popular manuals:

Dhyāni mudrā: sign of meditation, of mental concentration (also called the *samādhi* posture, *samādhi* being the culminating point of mental discipline). The posture, normally involving sitting Indian style, body upright, is represented with the two hands resting flat, one on top of the other, in the lap. In principle, this refers to the Attainment

of Enlightenment, but any meditation by the Buddha requires the same gesture….

Varada mudrā: sign of charity, generosity or favour, whether given or received (also called the *vara* mudrā, *vara* signifying choice, or a chosen object). The right arm is extended downwards, with the hand rotated outwards, palm open, fingers more or less straight.

Abhaya mudrā: sign of fearlessness (*bhaya* – fear, anxiety, fright, peril; *a* – a privative prefix). Following its etymology, the gesture can symbolize, collectively, 'one who has no fear at all'

(more specifically, at the time of the assault by the armies of Māra) and 'one who soothes, calms' (specifically, during the quarrel between the Koliyas and the Śākyas). The right forearm is bent at more or less of a right angle, the hand turned out to show the palm and the fingers straight and extending upwards.

Vitarka mudrā: sign of reasoning, of explanation (also called *vyākhyāna* – explanation, narrative). As a rule, the right forearm is bent, as above, but tends to be held closer to the body; the hand is held in the same manner but the fingers are slightly bent, and the index finger touches the thumb. The gesture can be made in a seated posture (Indian or European style) or standing. In the latter case, the left hand holds the edge of the garment or, from the Pāla-Sena period on, makes the same gesture as the right hand does, but points towards the ground….

Dharmachakra mudrā: sign of the Wheel of the Law (or better, *dharmachakra pravartana* mudrā – sign of the Setting in Motion of the Wheel of the Law). In accordance with its

designation, this is the gesture *par excellence* symbolizing the First Sermon ('Setting in Motion of the Wheel of the Law') delivered at Sārnāth, on the site of the Rishipatana (Pāli, Isipatana) in the Deer Park, but it can also refer to the 'great magical wonder' of Śrāvastī. Hence, the necessity for the artist to specify the scene symbolically or by a narrative. The gesture consists in bringing both hands in front of the torso, in the same movement as in the *vitarka* mudrā but with this modification: that the fingertips of the left hand come to rest against the palm of the right hand….

Bhūmisparśa mudrā: sign of touching the earth (also called *bhūsparśa*; *bhū* – earth), most often described as 'gesture of calling the (deified) Earth as witness', a reference to the Miracle consecrating the defeat of Māra, or the 'gesture of Māravijaya', the victory over Māra which is the precise and unique significance of this gesture, implying a notion of imperturbability. This mudrā, which can be made only by a figure

A Laotian Buddha in the 'calling the Earth as witness' posture.

seated Indian style, consists of lightly touching the seat with the fingertips of the right hand stretched out over the right thigh, more or less close to the knee; the left hand rests in the lap.

Jean Boisselier
La Grammaire des formes et des styles Asie, 1978

From the Buddhism 'of the Ancients' to Mahāyāna

Over the course of the twenty-five centuries since the Enlightenment, Buddhism has undergone many permutations and developed into distinct traditions. Yet all share certain beliefs about the Buddha's code for living.

多聞大王毗沙門比

四天王衆天之圖

天日神

大力神

天愛增

天遠擁護

天壬堅

海水青

After Mahāparinirvāṇa, the various communities, now bereft of the Buddha's own explanations of the Doctrine and not yet having written accounts of his words, tended to give the Teaching their own interpretations. It was in this way that the doctrines that developed into Mahāyāna Buddhism must have emerged, at roughly the same time as the beginning of the Christian era.

Meditation on the Three Jewels

Back in ancient times, Buddhism had Three Jewels – the Buddha, the Law (*dharma*) and the Order (*saṅgha*) – which it embraced with equal reverence. The Buddha is the all-knowing one who discovered the Holy Truths; the Law is the doctrine and the religious discipline he established; the Order, in its narrowest sense, is the monastic order founded by this same Buddha.

In the course of initiation and ordination ceremonies, laypeople and monks pledge adherence to the Three Jewels by declaring three times: 'I take refuge in the Buddha; I take refuge in the Law; I take refuge in the Order.' One cannot be an authentic Buddhist without engaging in this act of taking refuge (*śaraṇagamana*)....

The Three Jewels lead the list of commemorative subjects (*anusmriti*) on which the disciple is invited to meditate. These subjects number six, eight, or ten: 1. the Buddha; 2. the Law; 3. the Order; 4. rules of morality; 5. generosity; 6. heavenly beings; 7. inhalation and exhalation; 8. death; 9. aspects of the body; and 10. peace.

A Chinese engraving illustrating the world of the Dharma.

Calling to mind the Three Jewels is the best way to triumph over the fears that assail the solitary monk. This is what is stressed in several texts, most notably an old canonic sūtra entitled *Dhvajāgrasūtra* ('Sermon on the Banner's Pole')....

In these canonic sources to which we have just alluded, the Three Jewels are briefly evoked in a formula, identical, repeated over and over:

'It is he the Tathāgata, he who is right, correctly and fully awakened, gifted with knowledge and skill, the One Who Has Attained the Realm of Bliss, the master of the world, leader of the beings who tame those who are humans, instructor of gods and humans, the Buddha, the Blessed One.

'The Law was skilfully formulated by the Blessed One; it is rewarded in the present existence; it is independent of time; it demands that one come to examine it; it leads to a good place and should be known internally by the wise.

'The Order of disciples of the Blessed One follows the right path, follows the straight path, follows the path of the right method, follows the path of the right life.... This Order of disciples of the Blessed One is worthy of veneration, worthy of offerings, worthy to be acknowledged with hands joined; it is the supreme field of merits for the world.'

Just as it is, with all its repetitions and obscurities, over the course of centuries this formula has fuelled the piety of millions of Buddhists. It has withstood the ravages of time and still remains valid today. But the interpretation given to it has varied slightly depending on the time and the place.

This is because Buddhism, over the course of its long history, has taken twists and turns that have led to noticeable changes in its religious ideal, philosophical opinions and beliefs about the personhood of the Buddha himself.

Etienne Lamotte,
'Du Petit Véhicule au Grand Véhicule'
in *Le Bouddhisme,*
edited by Lilian Silburn, 1977

The Four Noble Truths

The Buddha's doctrine consists, as he himself formulated it in his First Sermon, of 'Four Noble Truths'. The first is the fundamental observation of the existence of suffering. Suffering exists in birth, sickness, death, encountering what is disliked, separating from what is liked, not obtaining one's desires, and in what is summed up by the five 'aggregates of attachment' (*upādānakkhandha*). This observation is not at all simple; in its final item, it finishes with a theoretical opinion connecting the painful nature of everything associated with the spiritual and physical being, as represented in the Doctrine, to the entire mass of things to which it becomes attached and which lead to repeated rebirths....

The truth about the origin (*sumudāya*) of this suffering is the second of the noble truths. It consists in 'thirst' – we would call it 'appetite' (*tanhā*). This takes three forms: thirst for sensual pleasure (*kāma*), thirst for existence (*bhava*), thirst for 'inexistence' (*vibhava*). The first is self-explanatory: desires are the cause of suffering because they cannot be satisfied indefinitely and also because they are connected to painful existence. The second focuses on a direct craving for these existences. The third is a craving for the void that, while having as its object the inverse of the former, is nonetheless a craving and, as such, is an act that brings about existence; suicide leads to rebirth.

The third truth concerns the dissolution (*nirodha*) of suffering which is the dissolution of the thirst generating rebirths, the craving associated with pleasure and passion, in which one searches willy-nilly for a super-pleasure.

The fourth truth stresses the 'path that leads to the cessation of suffering' (*dukkhanirodhagāminī patipadā*), called the 'eightfold path' [Pāli words are given in parentheses]:

1. Perfect view (*sammādiṭṭhi*)
2. Perfect resolve (*sammāsankappa*)
3. Perfect speech (*sammāvācā*)
4. Perfect conduct (*sammākammanta*)
5. Perfect livelihood (*sammāājīva*)
6. Perfect application (*sammāvāyāma*)
7. Perfect mindfulness (*sammāsati*)
8. Perfect concentration (*sammā-samādhi*)

Buddhist doctrinal description is easily arranged around these four truths. The Buddhist representation of the state of things in the world is what the first truth about the nature of suffering is based upon. This representation is a cosmology with regard to nature, and a physiology and psychology with regard to beings.

Jean Filliozat
L'Inde classique, 1953

Space is populated by innumerable universes

First of all, let us examine how the Buddha and his disciples represented the world, which so strongly resembles a prison. In a space that cannot be described as either finite or infinite, innumerable universes, all formed according to the same model, are distributed. At the bottom is the world of desire…. It has the shape of a cylinder with a vertical axis; on the upper circle live people, animals and the lower divinities. At the centre of the circle stands a tall mountain, Mount Meru, or Sumeru, around which revolve the sun, the moon and the other stars. On the periphery, a mountain chain hems in the ocean and prevents it from spilling into space. Four continents stretch from the foot of Mount Sumeru towards the four cardinal birth directions. The southern continent, Jambudvīpa, named after a tree, the jambu, or rose-apple, stands at the centre and is where India is located; it has the same triangular form as the latter. The northern continent, Uttarakuru, is populated by humans living in perfect harmony, in an idle state completely free from cares or troubles. The two other continents, to the east and west, are only names. Halfway up Mount Sumeru, or at its summit or above, live the gods of desire, in celestial palaces, notably those belonging to the old Vedic religion, over which Indra reigns, who in Buddhist texts bears the name Śakra. In the bowels of the earth or in the gaps between the universes live the damned, who undergo various tortures of an extraordinarily long duration – as long as the blessed life of the gods but, just as in the case of the latter, always finite.

Above the world of desire, at such a height that humans cannot dream of perceiving it, is the world of forms, inhabited only by gods of ethereal substance who are immersed in endless meditation. The four levels of this world correspond, in effect, to the four stages of Buddhist meditation. Through assiduous practice, monks can achieve the possibility of rebirth among

Bas-relief from a temple in Borobudur, Java.

these gods, among other advantages. The lower level is the dwelling place of Brahmā who, with Śakra (Indra), plays an important role in Buddhist legend. These gods of the world of forms are all purity and light, their diaphanous bodies without need to take in nourishment, and their thoughts free of the slightest guilty desire. Sheltered from the defilement of birth, they emerge spontaneously in the sky, without having a father or mother.

Above the world of forms, or in the further reaches of space, is the world without form whose four levels correspond to the four meditations known as immaterial. There live gods who have no bodies, pure spirits who, during the length of their lives of vertiginous duration, are absorbed in psychic states extremely close to total unconsciousness.

Such is the prison in which beings exist, changing stages with each death, passing from one to another of the five destinies – of the damned, of the ravenous shades wandering on or under the earth, of animals, of people and of gods. Here we see the Buddha's conception of what these beings were made of.

The impermanence of beings and things
Despite their extreme diversity, living beings have characteristics that they share with all inanimate beings, minerals, plants, ideas, mental functions, etc. In effect, all are composed and, as a consequence, conditioned. As such, they involve an act of production, a certain duration, a decline or alteration, and a cessation, which are the four common characteristics of composed things. All composed things have an origin and are prey to external conditions and causes. Everything that has an origin has, of necessity, an end…. The universe itself, although its duration may be extremely long, measured in billions of years, also passes through phases of creation, development and then decline and destruction – the agents of the latter being, in turn, fire, water, and wind. All beings, thus, are only a series of passing phenomena that follow upon and condition one another. Thus when

a person dies and is reborn in the body of an animal, the latter is not altogether different from the former because everything – body, life, mind, longevity, pleasures and troubles – has no other origin than the acts of the person who came before. There is between them a relationship analogous to that between the infant and the adolescent, the mature person, and the elderly person, who are not at all identical to one another yet are nonetheless not truly different.

Thus, the first characteristic of composed things is impermanence. And it is precisely because they are impermanent that they bring suffering.

A 7th-century Japanese wood sculpture of the Bodhisattva Avalokiteśvara.

It is because life, even the extraordinarily long one of the gods, finishes with death, that it is painful; because the beings and the things one loves are taken away by death; because every moment of happiness is threatened by separation, sickness, cares and anguish, that all existence brings suffering. Let us not forget that this second characteristic of composed things – thus of ourselves – was the first subject of the Buddha's great discovery, the problem that he sought to resolve.

As they bring suffering, composed things are likewise empty, that is, devoid of any stable element on to which one can grasp, or on which one might build eternal happiness, sheltered from the perpetual vicissitudes of existence.

André Bareau
En suivant Bouddha, 1985

How the Order split into factions

Even during the Buddha's lifetime, factions began to appear within some communities. Born out of petty disputes or out of hunger for power, they only increased after the Master's death, motivating the convocation of the first councils.

In the absence of a supreme authority to define and impose an orthodoxy, the Saṅgha soon divided into groups (*nikāya*), schools or sects entertaining different ideas about the interpretation of the Buddha's teachings and how they should be adapted to new circumstances. About twenty such groups emerged in this way, one after another, all true to ancient Buddhism and faithful to the principles of the Doctrine. Only one has lasted to our own day, the Theravādin, which still thrives in Sri Lanka and southeast Asia. Among the others, the most important were the Mahāsānghikas, the Vātsīputrīyas, the Sarvāstivādas, the Sammatīyas, the Mahīshāsakas, the Dharmaguptakas, the Lokottaravādins and the Pūrvashailas. These groups all disappeared more than ten centuries ago.

At the very beginning of the Christian era, a new form of Buddhism appeared, which grew at a rapid pace. It was called Mahāyāna, or 'Greater Vehicle', and pejoratively labelled the ancient form of Buddhism Hīnayāna, or 'Lesser Vehicle'. Disparaging the notion of the *arhant,* which it deemed egotistical, it instead encouraged the adept to follow the Buddha's own example in becoming, starting in this life, a bodhisattva, striving over the course of innumerable existences to carry the practice of the great virtues to their perfection (*pāramitā*) – in particular, that of generosity (*dāna*) and wisdom (*prajñā*).

Full of infinite compassion, bodhisattvas are always ready to run to the help of all beings, and in case of need, to abandon their own property and even their lives; they lead beings to Deliverance while forsaking their own. … Through their profound wisdom they understand the true character of things and beings – namely, the emptiness (*shūnyatā*) of their essential natures. In contrast to what is asked of the *arhant,* it is not at all necessary to be a monk to be a bodhisattva. While continuing to venerate the Buddha, the faithful masses have devoted passionate cults to bodhisattvas and call on them in case of need. The most famous of these saviours are Avalokiteśvara, the 'all-compassionate', and Maitreya, who is to be the next Buddha.

Probing 'wisdom's perfection' (*prajñāpāramitā*) quickly led Mahāyāna scholars to expand the doctrine in this new direction. Around AD 200, [the Buddhist philosopher] Nāgārajuna provided a solid foundation to the theory of universal emptiness by analyzing all notions of substance through an extremely subtle dialectic; thus emerged the Mādhyamika [Middle Way] era. Two centuries later, [4th-century Indian Buddhist philosopher] Asanga founded [the school of] Yogāchāra, or Vijñānavāda, establishing a complex system having as its foundation an absolute idealism – everything is nothing but thought, a conviction one arrives at through the assiduous practice of special yoga exercises.

During the 7th century, another form of Buddhism emerged, called Vajrayāna ('Diamond or Lightning Vehicle') or, more frequently, Tantrism, because its sacred books were called *tantras.* This discipline combines yoga practice with a highly complex ritualism, mixed with magic, involving the worship of a large number of divinities, buddhas and Bodhisattvas. Its esoteric doctrine is inspired by that developed by Asanga, from which it draws the most daring inferences, and was furthered by various sects that flourished until the disappearance of Buddhism from India.

This occurred around the 13th century, when Muslim armies invaded Bengal, the last Buddhist kingdom. In fact, following a long period of decadence, Buddhism was already foundering a bit elsewhere due to various causes that are still poorly understood, although chief among which must figure the expansion of Hinduism, which extended its hold little by little over the entire Indian civilization, including late Buddhism, depriving monastic communities of the necessary support from lay followers.

André Bareau
in Le Grand Atlas des Religions, 1988

Persistence and vitality of the Buddhism of the Ancients

Buddhism of the Ancients

In the beginning was the Buddhism of the Śrāvakas (Listeners), or the immediate disciples, whose religious ideal was to direct adepts away from universal suffering in order to lead them to nirvāṇa, and who, from a philosophical point of view, espoused the inexistence of the individual soul (*pudgalanairātmya*), seeing reality only as psychophysical phenomena of existence.

The Śrāvakas, whose origins go all the way back to the appearance of the Buddha Śākyamuni, made their way across the continent of India and soon split up....

This fragmentation is explained by geographic and religious reasons. But if the eighteen sects disagreed on secondary points of doctrine, discipline and, most particularly, on the manner of conceiving of the Buddha, all remained faithful to the earliest ideal: rapid attainment of nirvāṇa according to the path traced by Śākyamuni.

The eighteen sects have not all survived the hazards of time, but the Buddhism of the Śrāvakas persists up to the present. [Brought around 1160 to Sri Lanka at the behest of Sinhalese King Parākramabāhu I (1153–86), Theravāda, 'Doctrine of the Ancients', still flourishes in Sri Lanka, Burma, Thailand, Cambodia and Laos.] Its profession of faith in the Three Jewels – the Buddha, the Law and the Order – remains the same as it was twenty

centuries ago, still using the ancient formula.

The latter, to be fully understood, required elaborations. These were codified around the 5th century AD by the great Sinhalese master Buddhaghosa. In his commentaries on the old canonic writings, and particularly in his outstanding work the *Visuddhi-magga* ('Path of Purity'), the savant takes the above-mentioned formulas, explains them word by word, and clarifies them through textual quotations....

At the beginning of the Christian era, a new genre of Buddhism arose in juxtaposition to the Buddhism of the Śrāvakas: that of the bodhisattvas, or future Buddhas. In opposition to the former, which it terms 'Lesser Vehicle' (Hīnayāna), it claims for itself the title of 'Greater Vehicle' (Mahāyāna), that is, 'Great Means of Advancement'. This movement, which gave birth to an abundant literature, the Mahāyāna sūtras, still known as the Vaipulyasūtras ('Extensive Sūtras'), enjoyed rapid success in India before spreading through the entire Far East, Central Asia, China, Korea, Japan and Indochina.

The Bodhisattvas' role in Mahāyāna

As adepts of Mahāyāna, the bodhisattvas delay their own entrance into nirvāṇa and focus their efforts on the production of Awakened Thought (*bodhicittotpāda*). They resolve to one day achieve the Supreme Awakening experienced by Buddhas in order to consecrate themselves indefinitely to the good and happiness of all beings.

This Supreme Awakening – or Enlightenment, as it is sometimes called – consists in understanding all things not only in terms of their three general characteristics – impermanence,

The 8th-century Korean statues of the Buddha's 'thousand transformations'.

suffering and impersonality – but also under their innumerable aspects. This is not a matter of science but of omniscience, or universal wisdom.

In any case, according to Mahāyāna Buddhism, things are empty by their very nature and character and, in consequence, are free from any birth and any destruction. Not content to proclaim, as the Śrāvakas did, the impersonality of the psychophysical phenomena of existence, the bodhisattvas declare these phenomena to be absolutely nonexistent, or claim that they exist only in the minds of conscious subjects. In a word, according to this new point of view, the rejection of the notion of the individual (*pudgalanairātmya*) already professed by the Śrāvakas, should be matched by a rejection of the notion of things (*dharmanairātmya*). No longer seeing the world in terms of people or things does not in any way prevent the bodhisattva from devoting himself or herself to good and to universal happiness – because if this altruistic activity is doomed from a universal point of view (*paramārtha*), it is justified from a practical one (*samvriti*).

Bodhisattvas link a great facility in salvational means (*upāyakausalya*) to the wisdom that keeps them from seeing and conceiving, which makes them supremely benevolent.

Etienne Lamotte
in *Le Bouddhisme*, 1977

The expansion of Buddhism in Asia

Taught by monks wherever they travelled, the Buddha's Doctrine was open to a wide variety of interpretations and to the influences of local languages and cultural traditions. Then the new communities began to propagate the Doctrine into other lands.

The diffusion of Buddhism

In contrast to Hinduism, Buddhism is a missionary religion. One of its duties is to make a gift of the Law. Furthermore, it has never regarded just one language as sacred – as opposed to Hinduism, which preserves intact the ancient Sanskrit. Buddhist monks translated the Buddha's words into all the languages in which they preached; only the interpretation had to remain faithful. This is why Buddhism was able to spread throughout Asia in one of the most powerful movements of civilization that humanity has known....

From the beginning of the Christian era, starting in Kashmir, Buddhism reached the Greek kingdoms in the north of present-day Pakistan and Afghanistan. Greco-Buddhist art blossomed and there, for the first time, artists sculpted statues of the Buddha. Buddhism also reached the borders of the Iranian world and, following an important commercial current, the 'silk route', penetrated the oases of Central Asia, whose populations integrated Iranian, Indian and Hellenic cultures into a civilization of extreme refinement. There, Sanskrit studies were also of the first rank. From these regions, Buddhism could spread into China.

At the end of the 2nd century, Buddhist missionaries were active in Vietnam, a port stop on the sea route from India to China.... Buddhism was also travelling over land routes during this period.

Murielle Moullec
in *Le Bouddhisme*
edited by Lilian Silburn, 1977

A monk participating in a ceremony in Dharamsala, Tibet.

Chinese Buddhism

Buddhism, the only foreign religion to have as profound an impact on Chinese civilization, was transmitted and assimilated, essentially in its Mahāyāna form, during the course of a lengthy process that stretched from around the 2nd to the 8th centuries and was the product of several interactions: on the one hand, the arrival of foreign missionaries – coming from India, Parthia, Bactria, Sogdiana and the oasis-cities of present-day Chinese Turkestan – who flocked unremittingly towards a succession of capitals; on the other hand, the reactions to these teachings of the Chinese converts, who did not delay in establishing their own monastic communities, at first helping with translations, then developing their own interpretations and doctrines, then themselves travelling to Western regions to seek out more authentic traditions. There was also the reaction by supporters of the two major traditional systems, Confucianism and Taoism, and finally, the interplay of various political powers who sought to use these religions in the furtherance of their interests.

Traditional historiography maintains several versions of the arrival of Buddhism into China. The West has long known the story, clearly the most legendary, of the Emperor Ming of the Later Han [dynasty, 947–54]: the dream that he had of a 'golden man' who came to stand in the courtyard of his palace; the mission sent to the kingdom of the Yüeh-chih [Indo-Scythians]; the return to the capital Lo-yang with the two foreign monks, Kashyāpa Mātanga and Zhu Falan, who were installed in the Monastery of the White Horse, Baimisi.… All this took place around AD 67. This theory has been toppled by the moderns, who prefer another tradition admitting of an oral transmission of Buddhist texts by an envoy of this same Yüeh-chih kingdom in 2 BC in the capital of the time, Ch'ang-an. In any case, one can imagine a double source of penetration, one official, the other private, passing via osmosis between Western merchants and the Chinese over the course of centuries. Also, it was during the second half of the 2nd century that many translations took place.…

Chu Shih-hsing (3rd century) was the first Chinese to receive full monastic commandments. He died in Khotan while looking for sūtras, inaugurating a long line of Chinese monk-pilgrims, the list of the most well-known of whom includes Fa-hsien (died c. 420), I-ching (635–713), and especially Hsüan-tsang (602–64), who, after a long sojourn in India, brought back Yogāchāra, founded the Fa-hsiang school, revamped methods of translation and left a detailed account of his voyage, *Ta-T'ang-Si-Yu-Ki.*

The assimilation of Buddhism into Chinese thought occurred slowly. In the beginning, Buddhism profited from a kind of confusion with Taoism, reflected in the choice of the first texts to be translated, often practical treatises on meditation, similar to the 'internal alchemy'. The educated classes of the 4th century were fascinated with the concept of Emptiness (*kong*) in the *prajñāpāramitā* and wanted to apply the categories derived from Lao-tzu and Chuang-tsu to Buddhist exegesis; this was the practice of *ke-yi,* or 'matching the meaning', which, while it gave rise to a number of misunderstandings,

B uddhas sculpted in the rock of the Chinese
Yunkang caves around the 5th century.

allowed the implantation of Buddhism into educated milieux and into the general thought….

The introduction of Buddhism into China was revealed in a burgeoning of schools and sects: Tao-an (315–85), disciple of Fo-t'u-teng, organized a thriving community where exegesis and meditation (*dhyāna*) were practised; he was the initiator of the cult of Maitreya (Milefo), who was to play an important role in chan and popular religious beliefs…. Two great religious schools appeared under the Sui and the T'ang dynasties: T'ien-t'ai, based on the ideas of Chih-i (538–98), regarded as the founding patriarch) and of his master Hui-ssū (515–77), is a critical interpretation and a practice centred around the *Lotus Sūtra*…then the Hua-yen school, based on the *Buddhāvatmsaka-sūtra* and having as its patriarch and founder Fa-tsang, protégé of Empress Wu Hou (624–705)….

After the great persecution of the mid 9th century and the anti-foreigner reaction that followed the fall of the

Mongols during the Ming dynasty, Buddhism in its classical form became endangered; however, worship of Amitābha [Japanese Amida] continued in association with chan, a phenomenon that has continued up to the modern era. Scholarly thought made it syncretic with the 'three-doctrines-in-one' movement (*sanjiao guiyi*) that sought to unite Taoism, Confucianism and Buddhism into a single system.

Jean-Noël Robert
'Le Bouddhisme chinois'
in *Encyclopaedia Universalis*, 1985

Pursuing Enlightenment through meditation: Ch'an

It was in the Ch'an (*dhyāna*) school that Buddhism of Chinese inspiration showed all its capabilities. Ch'an concentrates on the practice of the internal life and above all on Enlightenment at the core of day-to-day activity. It disdains intellectual speculation and ritualism. It limits, when it does not exclude, recourse to Scripture. It is freely iconoclast, even blasphemous, not out of some theory, but because its aim is to achieve instantaneous Awakening by the shortest route, even if it is a brutal one.

A reaction against the Buddhism of the court, monastic opulence and the platitudes of the Pure Land [school], it advocated a return to simplicity and poverty, a passionate seeking, and an insistence on lived-life, daily behaviour separate from any theory, [a doctrine] reminiscent of early Buddhism. But, as a true Mahāyāna sect, its primary guiding interest is Enlightenment, awareness of nothing except that, teaching only that. After all, nothing else matters, and to attain it is simple enough. All that is needed is a zeal, an intuition, a perilous leap from the pinnacle, one more step when one is already standing at the topmost perch! The Ch'an master wants to instigate this act and nothing else; everything else that is given is extra....

In the importance that it accords to the free and spontaneous act, this sect, which is the most Chinese and the most advanced of the Greater Vehicle, rejoins ancient Buddhism. That the lesson of the Tao and its virtue is not at all foreign to it is certain but does not invalidate the observation that here and there, the Spontaneous is what is efficient.

Marinette Bruno
in *Le Bouddhisme*
edited by Lilian Silburn, 1977

Buddhism in Korea and Japan

Approximately one millennium after the death of the historical Buddha Śākyamuni, and a few centuries after the first evidence of Buddhism in China, this foreign religion started penetrating the islands of Japan by way of Korea. One of the main chronicles of ancient Japan, the *Nihonshoki,* compiled in AD 720 by imperial order, gives a detailed account of the event.

This official story of the arrival of Buddhism in Japan may be summarized thus. In AD 538, the thirteenth year of the reign of Kinmei-Tennō, 29th emperor of Japan, King Syong-Myong of the Korean state of Paikche, hoping to obtain an alliance against Korean states hostile to his own, sent a mission to Japan. With it he sent a gift to the emperor of a gold-plated bronze image of the Buddha Śākyamuni, as well as flags and umbrellas and several volumes of Buddhist sūtras. In a letter

A large 4th- or 6th-century sculpture of the Buddha discovered in a cave in China.

praising the merit of spreading the new religion, he called it the most excellent of all doctrines, pointing the way to the highest Enlightenment (*Bodhi*), although so difficult to comprehend that 'neither the duke of Chou nor Confucius had attained a perfect knowledge of it'. The letter concluded by citing the Buddha's alleged words: 'The Dharma shall be spread to the East.'

The emperor asked his ministers to advise him whether the new religion should be adopted. A conservative faction, represented by two powerful families, Nakatomi and Mononobe, was firmly opposed to the introduction of the 'foreign *kami*' (deity), as they called the Buddha. They feared that worshipping him would bring the wrath of the indigenous *kami* down on the nation. However, on the advice of the Soga family, who were in charge of foreign relations with Korea and one of whom, Iname no Sukune, held one of the highest governmental offices, the emperor decided that the image and the scriptures should be accepted and that the image should be 'tentatively' regarded as an object of worship. He entrusted the image of the Buddha to Iname no Sukune who, turning his house into a temple, enshrined it and worshipped it therein.

Those who dreaded the vengeance of the native deities proved to be justified in their fears: no sooner had the house of Iname no Sukune been transformed into a temple and the image worshipped there, than a horrible pestilence broke out in the country, causing the untimely death of a great many people.

As the disease became worse and worse, the emperor found no other way out of the calamity than to adopt the views of those who were opposed to the foreign religion: he had the Buddhist image thrown into a canal and burnt down the newly opened temple.

However, the following year, Kinmei-Tennō had two Buddhist images made out of a log of camphorwood which had been discovered floating upon the sea accompanied by miraculous voices singing Buddhist chants. During the next three decades, several monks, a nun, a sculptor and a temple architect arrived in Japan, bringing with them further Buddhist scriptures and images. The first Japanese nuns were ordained and more temples were built.

There were a number of setbacks during the reign of Emperor Bidatsu

(572–85) owing mainly to doubts about the new religion's efficacy as a means of preventing disease, and also to fear of the national *kami*. However, within only half a century Japan witnessed the firm establishment of Buddhism as a religion officially recognized and actively supported by the imperial court. The triumph of Buddhism over the factions hostile to its adoption was mainly brought about by the powerful Soga clan. They were strongly in favour of a policy of rapidly absorbing Chinese knowledge and ideas, since the Japanese state then emerging lagged far behind its mighty continental neighbour in culture and political organization.

Robert K. Heinemann,
'This World and the Other Power:
Contrasting Paths to Deliverance
in Japan',
in *The World of Buddhism*,
edited by Heinz Bechert and
Richard Gombrich, 1984

A Zen monk in Kyoto, Japan (opposite), and a Buddha in a cave in Korea (above).

Zen

The Zen school developed in China. A [6th-century] monk named Bodhidharma (Daruma, in Japanese), about whom little is known…is regarded as its founder. But it was Hui-neng (638–713), sixth patriarch of the school, who contributed most to its development. The term *zen* (*ch'an,* in Chinese), whose approximate translation is 'meditation', is an abrogated transcription that corresponds to the Sanskrit *dhyāna*.…

It was at the end of the 12th century, when Chinese Zen had already fragmented into several branches, that a Tendai [Japanese for T'ien-t'ai] monk named Eisai (1141–1215) came from Japan with the intention of improving his knowledge of esoteric cults. He became affiliated with a Zenist master of the Lin-chi branch and, after several years of study, returned to Japan and established there the Rinzai sect in 1191. Several years later, a monk named Dōgen (1200–53), who also had studied at Hien-zan and had become a disciple of Eisai, himself travelled to China. There he studied the Ts'ao-tung branch of Zen and, upon his return, in 1227, founded Japan's second Zen sect [Sōtō].

The Zen school invites us to see clearly what is inside us, which requires, accordingly, that our mind arrive at a state where it is 'empty' of what ordinarily fills it: space, time, affirmation or negation, good and evil. However, this state is lucid; the Japanese give it the name *satori,* which means 'knowing' in everyday language.…

The Zen schools, Sōtō in particular, suggest meditation in a seated position (*zazen*) sufficiently comfortable so that there are no distractions for the mind – because it should have none, even that of seeking to attain Enlightenment, which should happen all on its own. Another exercise in Zen consists in reflecting upon problems that seem on their surface absurd and that have no logical solution (*koans*). The masters are also in the habit of delivering blows to their students, even striking them with sticks. The point of these practices is the same: to put the disciple in a mental state in which his being is completely unsettled and becomes available to Enlightenment.…

It was chiefly in the countryside and in a relatively lower-class milieu that Sōtō developed. Rinzai, at least at the beginning, spread among the upper classes, in particular among the warriors of Kamakura and, later, of Kyoto, among whom it found great favour. The warriors were attracted by a religion said to have no need of books, ceremonies or prayers and that, on the other hand, required strong moral discipline.

Gaston Renondeau and Bernard Frank in *Présence du Bouddhisme,* 1987

Tibetan Buddhism

Introduced into Tibet in around the 7th century AD under royal patronage, Buddhism little by little won over all strata of the society and changed it profoundly. After Buddhism disappeared from India, Tibet became the centre of its dissemination and in its Tibetan form it conquered the whole of the Himalayan region, as well as Mongolia in the 16th century; it also had some influence in China, beginning with the Yüan.

In later sources describing the introduction of Buddhism at the time of what they call the 'first diffusion',

Tibetan silver-and-ivory prayer wheel.

legend has replaced history. Tibet's conversion was part of a divine plan whose tools were the dynastic kings. At the end of the 6th century, they had unified the land and undertaken

a remarkable programme of expansion; these kings were idealized, following the Indian model of the 'king who governs according to the Dharma'. As a consequence, conversion must have been rapid and massive under the direction of the numerous pundits invited to Tibet, of whom the two principal ones, Sāntarakshita and Padmasambhava (about whom little historical certainty exists), are considered the initiators of the two currents that created Tibetan Buddhism, Mahāyāna and Vajrayāna, or Tantrism….

During this period, Buddhism was introduced by royal decree, the first monastery – Samye – was constructed, and the intensive translation of canonic texts was undertaken, which necessitated the development of a vocabulary able to accommodate Sanskrit and Buddhist notions….

In the 9th century, the dynastic collapse led to the collapse of the ecclesiastical Buddhist structure that it patronized. Little is known about the survival of Buddhism in Tibet up to its resurgence in the 10th century, in what the Tibetans call the 'second diffusion'. …It was to put an end to deviant Tantric practices and to restore the purity of the Doctrine and Buddhist practices that the Guge king Ye-shes-'od decided to renew the ancient religious ties to the Indian world, where he sent students….

But the true Buddhist reformer was Atīśa (982–1054), the celebrated Indian monk invited by Ye-shes-'od's successor to western Tibet, where he arrived in 1042. Reserving his Tantric instruction for his close disciples, he preached Mahāyāna Buddhism and is particularly well known for restoring the rigours of monastic life. It was probably due to his influence that the dissemination of the cult of Avalokiteśvara, considered the patron saint of Tibet, took place. The bodhisattva's formula, his *mantra* – *om mani padme hūm* ['Oh, the jewel in the lotus'] – has been repeated ad infinitum on prayer wheels, flags, engraved stones and the lips of all Tibetans....

In the 16th century, the political power of the most recent school, that of the 'School of the Virtuous' (Gelugpa), founded by Tsongkhapa (1357–1419), took form. Drawing from treatises by Indian Buddhist philosophers and by Atīśa, in his key works he explained the principles of Mahāyāna and of the *tantra*s. He integrated the two approaches, following the ranking introduced by Atīśa, wherein Hīnayāna (Lesser Vehicle) is the path intended for those of moderate abilities, Mahāyāna (Greater Vehicle) is addressed to those of good capacity, and Vajrayāna (Tantrism) is the 'rapid way' reserved for those of superior intellectual and spiritual ability. The school is known as that of the New Kadampa [or Yellow Hat, from the colour of the monks' headdress].

Its success was rapid. Crossing over into the realm of politics, by the 17th century, it had established its domination over the entire land, under the leadership of the fifth reincarnation of a disciple of Tsongkhapa: the fifth Dalai Lama, according to the Mongolian title bestowed upon this lineage since the 16th century. With minor variations, the religious government established at that time, sometimes defined as a theocracy, continued up until the present-day exile of the fourteenth Dalai Lama under pressure by Communist China in 1959.

Anne-Marie Blondeau
'Le Bouddhisme tibétain'
in *Encyclopaedia Universalis*, 1985

Lamaism

Lamaism [Mahāyāna Buddhism of Tibet and Mongolia] has a very particular appearance, both because it stresses certain Tantric traditions and because it integrates a number of elements from beliefs that existed before its time (or that subsequently coexisted alongside it) in Tibet....

In Lamaism, strictly religious activity is reserved for the specialists – monks or hermits – and the faithful are restricted to asking for their intervention without, most often, being themselves able to be present at rites and ceremonies, which are long and complex, or even secret....

If nothing other is demanded of believers than to make gifts to the church, or of the poor than to lead a moral life in order to accumulate merits – in the hope that the next existence will be a better one; if it is enough that they go on pilgrimages, circle around sacred objects, light lamps in front of statues of divinities; or, again, recite sacred formulae (the *mantra*s) – which moreover can be done mechanically (thanks to the famous 'prayer wheels'); one nonetheless expects of these faithful that they do all this with belief, concentration and a certain effacement of the self, because it is faith that, more than anything else, renders these practices effective....

Meditation, the 'essential practice in this religion of monks', follows the model of Indian Tantricism, as do its yogic practices. It centres on one of the divinities of the burgeoning Buddhist pantheon (often the goddess Tārā, one of the most popular) and consists not only of invoking a god, but in 'creating' it mentally, making it surge forth out of the 'void' – generally by means of a syllable, which is [thought of as] the seed – specifying the most precise details of its appearance, such as they are described in the treatises.

While doing this, meditating subjects identify themselves with this divinity or create the divinity in themselves, and then project it before them, which is essential if the divinity is to be able to act for the good of others and not just for them. At its most profound, this practice – which can demand years of exercise – lends a quasi-objective reality to the divinity and one, it is said, that is available to all the senses.

Finally, it is necessary to be able to reabsorb the deity back into the Absolute and then to dissolve it there. In this way, the meditating subject acquires not only divine powers but he or she also has the experience of the creation and dissolution of the phenomenal world and – on a human scale – birth, death and the intermediary state of *bardo;* however, at the highest level, the ultimate unity of *samsāra* and nirvāṇa is realized.

A. Padoux
in *Le Bouddhisme*
edited by Lilian Silburn, 1977

Origins of Tantrism

The origins of the Tantric movement go fairly far back in time and appear to be linked to old magic and religious beliefs that were perpetuated in India and elsewhere....

The most celebrated figure in Indian Buddhist Tantrism is certainly [the 8th-century Indian monk] Padmasambhava. If his historicity is not in doubt it must be acknowledged that legend has so disfigured him, attributing to him the most extraordinary magical exploits,

that one can only barely make out the principal features of his existence. Born in Śambhala in Urgyen, of royal blood – son of Indrabhāthi himself according to some traditions – he was called to Tibet around 750 by the first Buddhist apostle to go to that land, none other than the Mādhyamika master Śāntirakshita, abbot of Nālandā....

By the end of the 8th century, the principal centre of Buddhist Tantrism was eastern India, Bengal, Bihar and Orissa, where, thanks to the protection and solid support of the Pala dynasty, this discipline flourished. Around the year 800, the king Dharmapāla founded the great monastery of Vikramashīla, not far from Nālandā, which it soon eclipsed, becoming the most important seat of Tantric studies....

Around 1200, eastern India was invaded by the Muslim hordes who burned the convents and massacred monks by the thousands, putting a brutal end to the last brilliant epoch of Indian Buddhism. However, the religion continued, although in a much-diminished form, in other regions of India. In Kashmir, protected from the Muslim invasions by its girdle of mountains, it remained active until the 14th century....

The 'Rapid Way'

At a certain point, starting in the early 8th century, most Tantric schools deliberately took a particular position that stood in opposition to previous Buddhist teachings: this was in the introduction of an erotic dualism that was soon to assume a major importance. From earliest times, the great Buddhist masters had denounced, often vehemently, erotic passion as the most powerful link keeping beings in

Ritual bell from a Tibetan monastery.

the transmigratory cycle, and they advocated the suppression of sexuality – the Vinayapitaka in particular – even in its most benign manifestations, insisting on absolute chastity of body, word and mind, which became one of the fundamental rules of the monastic condition; over the course of twelve centuries of history, there resulted a misogyny comparable to that of the Christian Fathers.

In contrast, Tantric thinkers saw sexual symbolism in everything to a degree, exalting the importance and value of the feminine element, and introducing a multitude of goddesses into the pantheon....

Of course, one can find in almost any religion this kind of erotic symbolism, above all in the case of mysticism, but Tantricism – Hindu as well as Buddhist – gave it a much greater importance than it had had anywhere else. Not only did this view quickly invade its art and literature, but, particularly in certain schools, it exercised a profound influence on worship....

The constituent elements of this pantheon are, on the one hand, the Buddhas and Bodhisattvas, on the other, a multitude of divinities, spirits and demons.... The Buddhas and Bodhisattvas are, for the most part, those of Mahāyāna Buddhism, but their relationships are strictly defined. At the upper level of this pantheon, we find five supreme Buddhas, called Jinas (vanquishers) or Tathāgatas.... These five Jinas emanate five Buddhas who appear among humans to teach them the Way of Deliverance and who are composed of bodies of magical creation (*nirmānakāya*)....

Positioned below these, yet fulfilling important functions, are numerous divinities of all sorts and ranks drawn directly from the Hindu pantheon and Indian folklore. Acknowledged by Buddhism from its beginning and playing a not insignificant role in its literature, they had until that time remained outside the field of proper Buddhist worship. Contrarily, Tantrism recognized their right to be the objects of the zeal of its adherents on the same level as the Jinas, the Buddhas, the Bodhisattvas and the Śakti.

André Bareau
'Le Bouddhisme indien'
in *Les Religions de l'Inde,* vol. III, 1966

Buddhism and the West

Adherents of Buddhism care less about winning converts than about sharing a method of discipline for the mind and guidelines for living. Buddhism has shown itself to be remarkably flexible, adapting to different regions, climates, peoples and cultures.

Two thousand years of incomprehension

For two thousand years, Buddhism was less ignored than misunderstood by the West. The first encounters happened very early but were individual and short-lived. An ancient Pāli text, the *Milindapañha,* relates conversations between one of the successors to Alexander the Great's generals, Greek king Menander (2nd century BC), and the Indian monk Nāgasena, whom he asks to explain Buddhism's principles. Instructed by him in the doctrines concerning the illusory character of the permanent self, *karma,* and the chain of reincarnations, the king is said to have enthusiastically adopted them....

In the 2nd century AD, the first of the great Christian apostles, Clement of Alexandria, a converted pagan who himself converted pagans, spoke of the Indian philosophers and mentioned the Buddha....

In 3rd-century Alexandria, a cosmopolitan capital that enjoyed an

This Italian Buddhist monk is indicative of Buddhism's global expansion.

exchange of ideas from all horizons, a celebrated monk, Ammonius Saccas – who claimed Origen, the brilliant Christian exegete, as a student, as well as Plotinus, the last of the great pagan philosophers – is said to have been an Indian missionary....

Then came oblivion. Not altogether, however, for in the 13th century, one of the most celebrated novels of the Middle Ages, *Barlaam and Josephat,* relates in a duly Christianized version the story of the Buddha such as it is described in the *Lalitavistara,* the classic Buddhist text. Philosophers have been able to reconstruct the genesis of this singular transposition.... At the end of the 13th century, Marco Polo, who had encountered Buddhism in Asia, was able to write: 'But it is certain, had he been baptized a Christian, he (the Buddha) would have been a great saint alongside Our Lord Jesus Christ.'

Then there was silence. A silence not to be broken except by erudite travellers who collected editions of Buddhist texts in Tibet and Nepal. At the beginning of the 19th century, translations followed.... By 1860, it was thought that enough was known to publish some introductions to Buddhism. They long provided an inexact image, if not a caricature, of it. They found in it only a destructive atheism, based on 'bizarre imaginings' and with a 'morbid aspiration towards nothingness'. It has since been observed that this incomprehension arose in part from the fact that Buddhism was making use of psychological elements that were not recognized in the West until the study of the unconscious by psychoanalysis.

Jacques Brosse
in *L'Actualité religieuse dans le monde,*
October 1993

A look at Buddhism around the globe

United States, Canada and Brazil
In the 1860s and 1870s, hundreds of thousands of Chinese immigrants came to the West Coast of America and Canada to work in the gold mines and on the railroads. After 1882, Japanese labourers followed. From 1868, significant numbers of Japanese and Chinese immigrants also came to work on the sugar plantations of Hawaii, which was annexed as an American territory in 1898. Asian immigration to California was halted in 1902, but continued in Hawaii, which thus became an important centre for the transmission of Buddhism to America....

Chinese religion kept a low profile in North America, though a Pure Land mission was active to some extent among the Chinese. Today, most temples are hidden away in Chinatowns in big cities. They mostly follow traditional syncretistic folk religion, though some are mainly Buddhist and/or Taoist....

Japanese immigrants have been more obviously active in religious matters, many coming from an area where the Jōdo-shin sect was strong. This sect was also the most active in sending out missions. In 1889, the priest Sōryū Kagahi arrived in Hawaii and established the first Japanese temple there.... In 1899, Sokei Sonada came to San Francisco and established the sub-sect on the continent as the North American Buddhist Mission. During the Second World War, this was re-organized as the Buddhist Churches of America, and became independent of its Japanese parent body. To help pass on its traditions, the Mission and then

THE BUDDHIST
CONGREGATIONAL CHURCH OF AMERICA
CÔNG ĐỒNG GIÁO HỘI PHẬT GIÁO VIỆT NAM TẠI MỸ
FOUNDED B.E. 2519 — JANUARY 30, 1976
THE WASHINGTON AREA
BUDDHIST TEMPLE FOUNDATION STONE
DEDICATED B.E. 2523 — MAY 6, 1979
DURING THE OVERSEAS VIETNAMESE BUDDHIST
SANGHA CONFERENCE

Through the railings, one can glimpse an estate in Washington, D.C., that was converted into a Buddhist temple by the Buddhist Congregational Church of America.

Church organized a Young Men's Buddhist Association (1900), Sunday Schools, Buddhist women's societies, and educational programmes. These Western-influenced activities had already begun to develop in Japan itself at this time. The title 'Church' indicates further Westernization, as does the style of religious service, which are held on Sundays, use organs and include the singing of hymns....

After the war, two institutes for training priests were established. One of the Church's members was an astronaut killed in the 1986 Challenger space-shuttle disaster and, in 1987, the US Defence Department allowed the Church to put forward chaplains to work in the military. In 1987, the Church claimed 170,000 adherents, with sixty-six clergy and sixty-three temples in the USA. Most adherents are of Japanese descent. In Canada, in 1985, the related Buddhist Churches of Canada had eighteen member Churches and a membership of around 10,000. In Brazil, there are now around 500,000 people of Japanese ancestry. Various sects of Buddhism are found among them: Zen, Jōdo-shin, Jōdo, Singon, Tendai and Nichiren, and Brazilian Buddhists, numbering between 100,000 and 200,000, are mainly of Japanese descent....

After the Second World War, an interest in Buddhism was developed by some American servicemen taking part in the occupation of Japan, and in the Korean and Vietnam wars, and by some of the young people who travelled overland to 'mystic' India and Nepal in the sixties and seventies. Tibetan refugees also soon started to share their tradition with people in North America and Europe. From 1975, refugees from Vietnam, Laos and Cambodia have come to the West, their numbers reaching 884,000 by 1985: 561,000 in the USA, 94,000 in Canada, 97,000 in France, 91,000 in Australia, 22,000 in Germany, and 19,000 in Britain....

Zen became the first form of Buddhism to really catch on among Caucasians, who found it very amenable to the pragmatic, energetic American disposition.

In post-war America, Zen continued to develop in the fifties 'Beat' period, and in the counterculture of the sixties and seventies, when Buddhism in general started to really take off, mainly in its Zen and Tibetan forms. While

A prayer service in the Buddhist Congregational Church of America in Washington, D.C.

Rinzai was the first form of Zen established in America, Sōtō, which is popular in Hawaii, followed. In 1961, the Sōtō master Shunryu Suzuki (1904–71) opened the impressive San Francisco Zen Center and, in 1967, established the Tassajara Mountain monastery. Sōtō Zen was also introduced by Reverend Master Jiyu Kennett, an Englishwoman born to Buddhist parents. After ordaining as a *bhiksuṇī* of the Chinese *Sangha* in Malaysia, in 1962, she went to Japan and trained as the only woman in a Sōtō temple. In 1969, she went to America and, in 1970, she founded Shasta Abbey, in California, as the headquarters of the Zen Mission Society. A mixture of Rinzai and Sōtō is also taught, as at the cluster of buildings which forms the Zen Center of Los Angeles, established in 1956.

The four main schools of Tibetan Buddhism are all present in the USA, attracting a growing number of young people by their mixture of mysticism, symbolism, ritual and psychological insights. Chogyam Trungpa Rinpoche (1939–87), a bKa'brgyud *bLama* [religious teacher], established a thriving centre at Boulder, Colorado, in 1971. This has since become the centre of the Vajradhātu organization, a network including many meditation centres, affiliated groups and a Buddhist Institute....

In the Chinese tradition, Buddhist groups have become more active and have attracted Caucasians. Tripiṭaka Master Hsuan Hua has been particularly influential. Coming from Hong Kong in 1962 at the invitation of some Chinese-American disciples, he founded the Sino-American Buddhist Association [SABA] in San Francisco in 1968. His reputation soon attracted Caucasian followers, who comprised two-thirds of the SABA membership by 1971. By 1977, the Association's headquarters was 'The City of 10,000 Buddhas', a large former hospital in extensive grounds, in northern California....

In 1960 the Sōka-gakkai, as 'Nichiren Shōshū of America', began to vigorously proselytize, starting in Los Angeles. Since 1967, it has worked beyond the Japanese-American community, so that 95 per cent of its members are now non-Asian. By 1970, it claimed 200,000 members in the USA, and by 1974, it had groups on over sixty university and college campuses. Its membership includes more Hispanics and Blacks than other Buddhist groups, and also media personalities....

The Theravāda tradition is still young in the USA, its first *vihāra* [monks' residence] being established by the Sinhalese in 1966 in Washington, D.C. Since then, others have been opened, and the tradition has started to flourish. Americans have ordained as monks and, from 1987, as ten-precept nuns, and meditation centres teaching Insight meditation are becoming popular....

Australia
In Australia, Buddhism arrived in 1882 with a small group of immigrants from Sri Lanka. It also existed among Chinese settlers. However, it did not start to develop among other sections of the population until the 1930s.

Africa
In Africa, a Buddhist monastery was established in Tanzania in 1927 by immigrant labourers brought over from Sri Lanka. It still exists, though the number of Buddhists seems to be dwindling. Immigrants from Sri Lanka also seem to be behind the existence of Mahā Bodhi Societies in Ghana and Zaire, and a Buddhist society in Zambia, where some among the indigenous population are now starting to express an interest in Buddhism.

From 1860 to 1913, low-caste Indians came as indentured labourers to South Africa, mainly to Natal. In the 1920s and 1930s, increasing discrimination led some of them to Westernize and convert to Christianity, while others explored their Indian roots, strengthening their Hinduism. Some turned to Buddhism, attracted by what they saw as its freedom from caste and superstition, its social ethic, and its emphasis on the compassionate Buddha-nature within all. Links with Buddhists in south India led to the founding of a Buddhist Society in 1917. It was never a mass movement, however, its weakness being that it has had no temples or monks; the recent interest in Buddhism among Caucasians may remedy this, though.

The United Kingdom
The first Buddhist missionary to Great Britain was Dharmapāla [a lay activist from Sri Lanka], who visited for five months in 1893, then in 1896 and 1904. On these occasions, he made contact with T. W. Rhys Davids, Edwin Arnold and Theosophists.... In 1907, the Buddhist Society of Great Britain and Ireland was formed, with T. W. Rhys Davids as its president, to receive

The figure seated in the centre of this group posed in front of Potala Palace, the seat of the Dalai Lama, is Alexandra David-Neel, who wrote some of the first French texts about Buddhism. Her face is blackened with soot in the traditional Tibetan manner.

a mission, and in 1908 Ānanda Metteyya [a Burmese-trained British monk] and three Burmese monks arrived in Britain.

The Society was interested in a modernist version of Southern Buddhism, as both a world-view and an ethic. At first, progress was slow, but from 1909 to 1922, the *Buddhist Review* was published. The First World War held up development, and afterwards the Society struggled on until it collapsed in 1924. In this year, however, the lawyer Christmas Humphreys (1901–83) founded the Buddhist Lodge of the Theosophical Society, which absorbed the remnants of the previous Society in 1926. In 1943, the lodge became the Buddhist Society, and its journal (*Buddhism in England*) became *The Middle Way,* which is still going strong....

From the seventies, Buddhism started to put down firm roots, as seen by a more widespread commitment to Buddhist *practice,* as opposed to a still mostly intellectual interest, and by the development of a social dimension, with the establishment of an indigenous *Sangha* and many Buddhist centres. The strongest traditions are Theravāda, Tibetan, Zen, and a syncretistic group known as the Friends of the Western Buddhist Order....

The growth of Buddhist monasteries and meditation centres has helped stimulate something of a revival in Christian meditation, and Christian monks and nuns sometimes learn techniques from Buddhist ones. Besides Asian Buddhists, there are probably between 10,000 and 100,000 Buddhists in Britain....

Continental Europe
In Germany, interest has long been focussed on the Southern tradition, which perhaps appeals to those from a Protestant culture. The first Buddhist society was started in 1903 by the Pali scholar Karl Seidenstüker, to promote Buddhist scholarship. Success was

Buddhist prayers in France, at a site near the Vézère River in Dordogne.

small, though. An influential figure in early German Buddhism was George Grimm (1868–1945), whose *The Doctrine of the Buddha, the Religion of Reason* (1915, in German) was one of the most widely read books on Buddhism, both in its original German, and in many translations. His interpretation of the *Suttas* saw the teaching that all phenomena are not-self as a way to intuit the true Self, which lies beyond concepts. As he felt that the Buddhist tradition had misunderstood the Buddha, he called his interpretation 'Old Buddhism', meaning 'original' teaching.… Another key Buddhist was Paul Dahlke (1865–1928), who developed an interest in Buddhism while in Sri Lanka in 1900. He followed a modernist version of Southern Buddhism, well-rooted in the Pali sources. He built the 'Buddhist House' in Berlin-Frohnau, a temple/meditation-centre opened in 1924, and also published translations of a number of *Suttas*.…

[The situation] changed after the Second World War, especially due to the influence of a small book by Dr Eugen Herrigel. This was *Zen in the Art of Archery* (1948, in German), the fruit of five years of studying a Zen martial art. From the seventies, Zen centres have sprung up, and Jōdo-shin also established a presence. The post-war period also saw the introduction of the Arya Maitreya Mandala, which had centres in ten cities by 1970. This is a lay Order founded by *bLama* Anagārika Govinda (1898–1985), a German who had trained in both the Southern and Northern traditions, and was a follower of the Tibetan ecumenical *Ris-med* movement. From the seventies, other

Tibetan groups have been established.

France has been strong in Buddhist scholarship. Its first Buddhist society was 'Les Amis du Bouddhisme', founded in Paris in 1929 by the Chinese reformer T'ai-hsu and Constant Lounsberry. There are now many refugees from Indo-china living in France, who had set up three Vietnamese temples by 1984. The strongest tradition, with forty-six centres by 1984, was the Tibetan one, with Zen having five centres, and the Theravāda two, along with two monasteries....

In Italy, only a few Buddhist groups existed by 1970, but in 1986, there were over thirty centres and monasteries, and approximately twenty-five societies, mainly Tibetan and Zen.

The *International Buddhist Directory,* giving information for 1984 listed Buddhist organizations in Austria, Belgium, Denmark, Finland, Greece, Holland, Norway, Portugal, Spain, Sweden and Switzerland. In Western Europe as a whole, excluding the United Kingdom, it listed: 139 centres, one monastery, and one Institute of the Tibetan tradition; thirty-four centres and two monasteries of the Zen tradi-tion, and twenty-five centres and two monasteries of the Theravāda tradition. The Jōdo-shin school has two temples in Switzerland and one in Belgium. In 1987, a two-year-old Spanish boy, son of a couple running a Tibetan Buddhist centre in Spain, was recognized as the reincarnation of Thubten Yeshe Rinpoche (1934–84), a dGe-lugs *bLama* who had been very active in establishing Tibetan centres and monasteries in the West. The boy now resides as spiritual focus of Kopan monastery, Nepal, which was established by *bLama* Yeshe.

A Buddhist Union of Europe was formed in 1975, as a common forum for discussion, co-operation, publications, and liaison with psychological and medical institutes. By 1987, it included national Buddhist Unions of Austria, France, Germany, Italy, Holland, and Switzerland, and around fifty organizations (such as the London Buddhist Society), monasteries and groups. In 1987, it claimed that there were over a million Buddhists in Europe (including Asians). Besides 500,000 claimed for England (a figure which is far too high), other figures given were: 70,000 in Germany, 200,000 in France, 15,000 in Italy, and 6,000 in Austria.

B. Peter Harvey
An Introduction to Buddhism, 1990

This young Spanish boy is believed to be the reincarnation of a Tibetan missionary lama.

A conversation with the Dalai Lama

Recipient of the 1989 Nobel Peace Prize, the current, fourteenth Dalai Lama (b. 1935) smilingly describes himself as a 'politician despite myself'. Exiled from Tibet, his homeland, since 1959, he radiates harmony with the world and within himself.

Could you describe how you understand Buddhism? Is it a religion, a practice or a philosophy?

It's all three at once. In it, one practises various forms of meditation. And analytic meditation – among others – is done with the help of a certain knowledge. It's equally a religion, because this practice and this philosophy join beings together towards enlightenment, the refuge, helping them to become buddhas, enlightened beings.

The God of the Jews, Christians and Muslims to whom the faithful address themselves is a person, with whom one can have an actual exchange. It is also the 'All'. To you, does the Buddha correspond to this definition?

No. For us, the Buddha is not an 'All'. But if one defines God as a refuge, the Awakener, the Buddha corresponds to your idea of God. He is the omniscient Being *par excellence*.

On the other hand, he is not the creator of the world and its creatures. We believe that we all have the Buddha nature in us. Yet we cannot create ourselves.

So, in effect, the idea of creation is not at all understood in the same way in Christianity and in Buddhism?

For Buddhists, it is *karma* that creates the world. All action flows from a previous action, every event flows from a previous event, following the law of

T he fourteenth Dalai Lama.

causality. The strength of the mind, the sentiments, the emotions create the world in which we live, fashion beings....

Does human history have true importance for a Buddhist? Does the Buddha intervene in people's lives?

One must first of all clarify that to seek detachment from things does not mean to be disinterested in them. Even if I am a monk before everything else, I am interested in the events that take place in the world....

I believe, however, that there are several degrees of detachment and that fundamentally Buddhism calls for total detachment. For us, in effect, human history does not have the same importance as it does for you. And the Buddha would never intervene directly because we believe in the law of *karma*....

The Buddha's Four Noble Truths revolve around the question of suffering. Are not all religions different responses to the same question?

Suffering is indeed present from birth to death in human life, if it is only the moment that one of these stages is occurring. And I believe that without religion, without practice, it is difficult to eliminate, to come to terms with, suffering. Beyond this, the totality of Buddhist teaching tries to teach how to eliminate all sources of suffering, to liberate oneself from them. Christianity also offers to help people in accepting, in preparing for, death. But religions show a path. Each one is free to follow it or not....

Millions of Westerners are attracted by the Dharma [Buddhist Law]...and because of this are losing interest in their own tradition.

There are two phenomena. Some people maintain their faith in their religion of origin and adopt certain techniques, certain practices, from another religion. I believe that this is very positive. But other people wish to change religions. It is this phenomenon that is the most dangerous.

People should think long and hard about this – because it is not natural to cut off one's roots. If it is done too rapidly, it is generally out of bitterness and disappointment with one's old religion. Then one becomes a critic of one's religion of origin. This is very serious because one destroys the very spirit of religion, which is its tolerance, wisdom, love....

Do you believe that Buddhism can become fully transplanted in the West?

If one looks at Buddhism's history, one must distinguish between the Buddha's essential teachings and culture. The basic teachings, spreading throughout the world, have taken root in diverse cultures. That is why one speaks in terms of Tibetan Buddhism, Chinese Buddhism, Thai Buddhism, etc. In view of this history, one can say that it is altogether possible that the basic teachings will anchor themselves in Western culture and that one day a Western Buddhism will exist.

Interview by E. Saint-Martin in *L'Actualité religieuse dans le monde*, November 1993

GLOSSARY

Entries are in Sanskrit unless otherwise noted.

abhaya ('safety; peace') One who has no fear, who reassures. The *abhaya mudrā* is the gesture of assuagement

arhant ('deserving') A venerable, saintly being who has reached the fourth stage on the path of deliverance, who has attained nirvāṇa in the present life and will never again be reborn, having been exhausted of all passions and faults

ātman ('self') A reflexive pronoun that designates the principle of individuality of each being and each thing (denied in Buddhism)

Avalokiteśvara ('the master who looks towards the earth') One of the chief Bodhisattvas of the Mahāyāna tradition

bodhi ('awakening') The principle discovery of the Four Noble Truths; the 'coming into consciousness' through which a Bodhisattva arrives at Buddhahood

Bodhisattva ('a being on the path of Enlightenment') A future Buddha

Brahman The sacred, 'ritual word', principle of being, the universal 'self' that the principal Brahmanic sect identifies with the individual 'self'

brāhman Devotee or priest; possessor of the Veda

Buddha ('awakened [or enlightened] one') One who has discovered the Four Noble Truths and has thus attained nirvāṇa in this world

cakra ('wheel') A wheel, circle or disk; symbol of the Buddhist Law; emblem of sovereignty

cakravartin ('one who possesses the Wheel') A Universal Monarch guided by the Law he teaches

dharma ('order, rule, law') The notion of holding or grasping, of existing – from whence comes its designation as defining Buddhist doctrine; the natural laws to which things and beings are subject; phenomena or things ordered by these laws, that is, things understood as mental objects

dhyāna ('meditation, absorption') An advanced stage of consciousness

Jātaka ('birth') The collection of approximately 547 stories of the Buddha's prior existences – as animals, divinities and humans

jina ('victor') An epithet used for the Buddha, saints of Jainism and sometimes for Vishṇu

karma ('deed') An act that has moral significance – good, evil or neutral

Maitreya ('the benevolent') Name of the next Buddha to come

mantra A verbal formula repeated as a form of meditation

mudrā ('seal, sign') A codified bodily gesture having specific iconographic significance – in Tantrism, one full of mystical value and magic

nirvāṇa ('extinction') The unchanging, ineffable state obtained by the absence and cessation of all desire; cessation, a state of deliverance achieved by Buddhas and arhants

pāramitā ('perfection') One of the virtues practised to perfection by Bodhisattvas

Parinirvāṇa ('total extinction') The death of a 'perfectly and completely Enlightened' Buddha; the definitive disappearance of all the elements and phenomena, material and spiritual, that went into forming his being; after this, the Buddha will never be reborn

prajñā ('wisdom, intelligence') Ability to know and understand

Prajñāpāramitā ('perfection of wisdom') Mahāyānist doctrine personified by the feminine form of a Bodhisattva, presented as the spiritual mother of all the Buddhas

samsāra ('journeying, transmigration') Ancient Indian doctrine concerning the succession of births and rebirths

Saṅgha ('crowd, host') The Buddhist monastic community

stūpa Characteristic Buddhist monument derived from funerary tumuli; a tower, usually bell-shaped, that houses the relics of the Buddha or one of his disciples

sūtra ('thread') Text or discourse containing a sermon of the Buddha or one of his disciples

tantra ('weft; context; continuum') One of a set of mystic and magical scriptures, sometimes involving secret rites, that accord particular emphasis to the feminine energy associated with the masculine divinity; arising as a movement in the 6th century, Tantrism penetrated both Brahmanism and Buddhism

tathāgata A word of controversial meaning: 'thus-come or thus-gone one', etc; one of the Buddha's principle designations

ūrnā ('wool') Tuft of hair between the eyebrows of the Buddha; one of the 'bodily marks of the great man'

usṇīsha ('turban') In Buddhist iconography, the cranial protuberance on the Buddha's head; one of the 'bodily marks of the great man'

wat (Thai: 'temple') A group of structures constituting a Buddhist monastery in Thailand, Cambodia, or Laos

yoga ('yoke') The ability, care and concentration of the mind, and the power that results; philosophical system or religious practice

CHRONOLOGY

*For the earliest events, two sets of dates are given: traditional (**boldface**) and according to modern historians.*

543 BC/c. 425 BC	The Buddha's Total Extinction at Kuśinagara
542/c. 485	First Buddhist Council held at Rājagṛiha to establish the canon; the Buddha's chief disciple Mahākāśyapa leads five hundred arhants in a recitation of the Law and the Discipline in unison
443/c. 385	Second Buddhist Council at Vaiśālī, held to counter illicit practices adopted by the Vaiśālī monks
c. 6th–4th centuries	Establishment of the oral tradition of the Buddhist canon
c. 321	Maurya dynasty of northern India founded by Candragupta (d. c. 297 BC)
c. 273–32 (or c. 265–38)	Reign of Candragupta's grandson, Aśoka, a zealous supporter of Buddhism; Buddhist missionaries sent by Aśoka to regions bordering the Mauryan empire
c. 250	Third Buddhist Council convened at Pāṭaliputra; Mahinda (Aśoka's son or another close relative) arrives in Laṅka (Sri Lanka); conversion of the sovereign and his subjects
1st century BC	Theravāda Buddhist writings compiled in Laṅka (in Pāli); beginnings of the Mahāyāna school of Buddhism
1st century AD	Buddhist activity in Gandhāra and Afghanistan and expansion towards Central Asia and China
c. 150–250	Nāgārjuna, founder of the school of Mādhyamika ('the Middle Way')
320–7th century	Gupta dynasty in India, launched by Candra Gupta I (reigned 320–c. 330)
late 4th century	Asanga founds the Yogācāra school of Buddhism; introduction of Buddhism into Korea
399–413	Chinese pilgrim Fa-hsien visits India
440	Nālandā monastery, the future major (Mahāyāna) Buddhist university, founded by King Kamara Gupta I
5th century	Traces of Theravāda Buddhism appear in Burma and Thailand; cult of Amitābha (Amida) emerges in China
6th century	The Mahāvamsa, Pāli chronicle of Buddhist history in India and Sri Lanka, set in writing; introduction of Buddhism into Japan by Korean monks
late 6th century	Prince Shokotu promotes Buddhism in Japan
6th–7th centuries	In China, the T'ien-t'ai, Hua-yen and Ch'an (Zen) schools founded
629–48	Chinese pilgrim Hsüan-tsang travels to India
8th century	Mahāyāna and Tantric Buddhism penetrate Indonesia and the central zone of the Indochinese peninsula
845	Chinese emperor Wu-tsung begins a major persecution against Buddhism
12th–13th centuries	In India, penetration of Islam eliminates Buddhism, which continues to exist only in southeast Asian regions; in Japan, Zen and Pure Land sects founded
late 13th century	Rulers of north (Chiang Mai) and northeast (Sukhothai) Thailand adopt Theravāda Buddhism
14th century	Theravāda Buddhism adopted in Cambodia and Laos
1357–1419	Tsongkhapa, Tibetan Buddhist reformer and founder of the Dge-lugs-pa (or Gelugpa, 'Yellow Hat') order
after 1432	In Cambodia, the Vishnuite temple Angkor Wat, founded in the 12th century, becomes a Buddhist centre
1950	World Fellowship of Buddhists (WFB) founded; first WFB world conference held in Sri Lanka

FURTHER READING

Addiss, Stephen, *The Art of Zen: Paintings and Calligraphy by Japanese Monks, 1600–1925,* 1989

Bareau, André, *En Suivant Bouddha,* 1985

Bechert, Heinz, and Richard Gombrich, eds., *The World of Buddhism,* 1984

Boisselier, Jean, *Grammaire des Formes et des Styles: Asie,* 1978

Conze, Edward, *Buddhism: Its Essence and Development,* 1951

———, *A Short History of Buddhism,* 1982

Conze, Edward, ed., *Buddhist Scriptures,* 1959

Cowell, E. B., ed., *The Jātaka, or Stories of the Buddha's Former Births,* 1973

Cunningham, Alexander, *Mahābodhi,* reprint of 1892 ed.

David-Neel, Alexandra, *With Mystics and Magicians in Tibet: Magic and Mystery in Tibet,* 1984

De Bary, William T., *The Buddhist Tradition in India, China and Japan,* 1972

The Dhammapada, trans. by Nārada Thera, 1978

Filliozat, Jean, *L'Inde Classique,* 1953

Fischer, Robert E., *Buddhist Art and Architecture,* 1993

Harrer, Heinrich, *Lost Lhasa: Heinrich Harrer's Tibet,* 1992

Harvey, B. Peter, *An Introduction to Buddhism: Teachings, History and Practices,* 1990

Humphreys, Christmas, *Buddhism: An Introduction and Guide,* 1990

Humphreys, Christmas, ed., *The Wisdom of Buddhism,* 1987

L'Inde du Bouddha Vue par des Pèlerins Chinois, 1968

Kapleau, Philip, *The Three Pillars of Zen: Teaching, Practice and Enlightenment,* 1989

The Lalitavistara, or Memoirs of the Early Life of Śākya Siṅha, trans. by Rajendralāla Mitra, 1882

Lamotte, Etienne, *Histoire du Bouddhisme Indien des Origines à l'Ère Śaka,* 1958

Lee, Sherman E., *A History of Far Eastern Art,* 1989

Pal, Pratapaditya, *The Art of Tibet,* 1990

Rahula, Walpola, *What the Buddha Taught,* 1990

Les Réligions de l'Inde, 1966

Renondeau, Gaston, and Bernard Frank, *Présence du Bouddhisme,* 1987

Rhys-Davids, Caroline A. F., *Stories of the Buddha, Being Selections from the Jātaka,* 1989

Schumann, Hans Wolfgang, *The Historical Buddha: The Times, Life and Teachings of the Founder of Buddhism,* trans. by M. O'C. Walsh, 1989

The Shambhala Dictionary of Buddhism and Zen, trans. by Michael H. Kohn, 1991

Shearer, Alistair, *Buddha: The Intelligent Heart,* 1992

Silburn, Lilian, ed., *Le Bouddhisme,* 1977

Sivaramamurti, Calambar, *The Art of India,* 1977

The Sutta-Nipāta, trans. by H. Saddhatissa, 1985

Suzuki, D. T., *Zen and Japanese Culture,* 1982

Thomas, Edward J., *The Life of Buddha: As Legend and History,* 1975

Tucci, Giuseppe, *The Religions of Tibet,* trans. by Geoffrey Samuel, 1988

The Pāli Text Society (London) has published a 136 volume series containing the Pāli canon in its entirety.

LIST OF ILLUSTRATIONS

The following abbreviations have been used: *a* above; *b* below; *c* centre; *l* left; *r* right.

COVER

Front The Buddha with a halo, seated on a lotus. Detail from a Tibetan painting illustrating the Buddha's life, c. 19th century. Musée Guimet, Paris
Spine The Buddha standing, making a gesture of pacification. Ivory sculpture, Thailand, 19th century. National Museum, Bangkok
Back The Buddha 'making a witness of the earth'. Stone carving from Bihar, India, 6th or 7th century

OPENING

1 Prince Siddhārtha leaving his wife and son. Copy of a painting from Wat Rajasiddharam, Thonburi, Thailand, c. 1831
2 The god Indra playing a three-stringed lute. Copy of a painting from Wat Rajasiddharam, Thonburi, Thailand, c. 1831
3 Sujātā preparing a bowl of boiled rice for the Bodhisattva. Copy of a painting from Wat Dusitaram, Thonburi, Thailand, c. 1831
4 The nāga Mucalinda protecting the Buddha. Copy of a painting from Wat Dusitaram, Thonburi, Thailand, c. 1831
5 'The happy group of five' becoming the Buddha's disciples. Copy of a painting from Wat Dusitaram, Thonburi, Thailand, c. 1831
6 The Buddha performing the 'twin miracles'. Copy of a painting from Phra Thinang Buddhai Sawan, Bangkok, c. 1795
7 The Buddha visiting his father's palace. Copy of a painting from Wat Rajasiddharam, Thonburi, Thailand, c. 1831
8 The Buddha attaining nirvāṇa. Copy of a painting from Wat Rajasiddharam, Thonburi, Thailand, c. 1831
9 The brāhman Droṇa distributing the Buddha's relics. Copy of a painting from Wat Dusitaram, Thonburi, Thailand, c. 1831
11 The Buddha seated before a begging bowl. Mural painting, Sri Lanka, 18th century

CHAPTER 1

12 Lake Anavatapta in the Himalayas. Trai Phum manuscript of the Ayutthaya school, Thailand, 17th century. National Library, Bangkok
13 The god Vishnu on the primordial ocean. Indian miniature. Private collection
14 Female statue found at Mohenjo-Daro, 3rd-millennium BC Indus civilization. National Museum of Pakistan, Karachi

14–5 Reconstruction of Mohenjo-Daro. Archaeological Museum of Mohenjo-Daro, India
15a and 15b A zebu (Indian ox) and a mythical animal. Seals from the Indus civilization. National Museum of Pakistan, Karachi
16a The Vedic god Agni. Sculpted charcoal from India, 17th century. Musée Guimet, Paris
16b Ritual offering by a brāhman. Miniature from Deccan, India, 17th century
17 Indra with a Thousand Eyes. Mural painting, Puthenchira Temple, Bradakal, India
18 Sandstone sculpture in the Koh Ker style, Cambodia, early 10th century
18–9 The Nāga. Bronze sculpture from Cambodia, 12th century. Musée Guimet, Paris
19a Winged spirit. Bas-relief of the Śuṅga period, India, 2nd century BC. National Museum of India, New Delhi
19b Vishnu reclining on the serpent Ananta. Miniature of the Kangra school, India, 17th century. Private collection
20a A renunciant. Miniature of the Pahari school, India, c. 1700. Private collection
20b An ascetic. Sculpture from Mahābalipuram, India, 7th century
20–1 Yogis accomplish yoga postures. Indian miniature, Mewar school, 7th century
22–3 Gandhamādana, a mythical region in the Himalayas. Mural painting from Wat Suthat, Ratanakosin school, Bangkok, 19th century
24 and 25l Depiction of the universe according to Buddhist cosmography. Painting on paper, *The James Low Album of Thai Paintings*, c. 1820. Department of Oriental Manuscripts and Printed Books, British Library, London
25r Mahākāla. Painting on silk, Tibet, 18th century. Musée Guimet, Paris

CHAPTER 2

26 A Bodhisattva. Mural painting discovered in a cave in Ajantā, India, 6th century
27 Prince Siddhārtha taking an excursion in his carriage. Bas-relief from Borobudur, Java, 9th century
28 An elephant being led by monkeys. Medallion from the Bhārhut (India) stūpa, 2nd century BC. Indian Museum, Calcutta
29l The brāhman Sumedha (the Bodhisattva) laying out his hair for the Buddha Dīpaṅkara to walk upon. Shale bas-relief, Gandhāra school, Pakistan, c. 3rd century. Musée Guimet, Paris
29r Maitreya, the future Buddha. Shale sculpture, Gandhāra school, Pakistan, c. 2nd or 3rd century. Musée Guimet, Paris
30a The Bhojājāniya Jātaka (the Bodhisattva born as a horse). Engraved slab from Wat Si Chum, Sukothai, Thailand, 14th century. National Museum, Bangkok
30b and 31 The Sāma Jātaka. Painting, Thailand, early 19th century. Musée Guimet, Paris

CHAPTER 3

INDEX

Page numbers in *italics* relate to illustrations or references in captions.

ACKNOWLEDGMENTS

The author and publishers would like to thank Madeleine Giteau, Madame Jean-Louis Nou and Nathalie Hay for their help in the production of this work. Special thanks go to Natasha Eilenberg for her tremendous assistance in the preparation of the English-language edition.

PHOTO CREDITS

Martine Aepli 167. Alexandra David-Neel Foundation, Digne 177. All Rights Reserved 1–9, 44, 50, 52, 55a, 55b, 56b, 57, 62–3, 64–5, 66–7, 71, 81a, 84l, 85, 86–7, 90–1, 102, 103, 115b, 116, 151, 153, 158, 164, 168, 171, front cover. Artephot 41a. Artephot/Babey 26, 32–3, 78–9a, 78–9b. Artephot/Lavaud 32r. Artephot/Mandel 46, 142. Artephot/Nimatallah 28, 36–7, 87, 92, 97b, 100. Artephot/Percheron 144. Artephot/Roland 39a, 125r, 131. Jean Boisselier 95r. British Library, London 24, 25l, 50–1, 113, 116–7, 118a, 118–9, 136, 154. British Museum, London 47, 74, 75b, 80, 118b. Dagli-Orti, Paris 138. Edimedia 78, 110, 117a. Explorer/Tovy Adina 123a, 126–7. Explorer/Geopress 60, 106–7, 123b. Explorer/Krafft 27. Explorer/Jean-Paul Nacivet 36. Explorer/Jean-Louis Nou 83a, 88. Explorer/Ph. Roy 128. Explorer/A. Thomas 124. Explorer/Weisbecker 122a. M.G. 84r, 95l, 109b, 119. Giraudon 49a, 72, 120r. Giraudon/Bonora 16a, 77. Giraudon/CBO 14, 15a, 15b, 76, 149. Giraudon/Invernizzi 30a, 51, 53, 58, 59, 70b, 75a, 92–3, 94, 148, back cover. Giraudon/Lauros 19a. Marcel Giuglaris 161. Hanz Hinz, Basel 12, 22–3, 34, 34–5, 89, 102–3, 104a, 104b, 105, 114, 115a, 150. Information Ministry of the Government of India 130. Magnum/Bruno Barbey 165. Magnum/René Burri 129, 166. Magnum/Martine Franck 178. Magnum/Raghu Rai 162, 180. Jean-Louis Nou 11, 29r, 39b, 45b, 56a, 61a, 61b, 68l, 68r, 69, 70a, 82, 86, 98, 99, 106, 109a, 110–1, 112, 117b, 121a, 121b, 137, 146–7, spine. Rapho/Michaud 13, 14–5, 16b, 17, 19b, 20a, 20b, 20–1, 38–9, 41b, 54–5, 72–3, 97a, 120l, 122b, 134–5. Réunion des Musées Nationaux, Paris 18, 18–9, 25r, 29l, 30b, 31, 32l, 42–3, 45a, 48, 49b, 58–9, 83b, 91, 96–7, 100–1, 108, 125l, 127, 138–9. Roger-Viollet, Paris 157. Sipa Press/EFE 179. Sipa Press/Guadrini 172. Sipa Press/Trippett 174, 175

TEXT CREDITS

Grateful acknowledgment is made for use of material from the following works:
(pp. 136–8) E. B. Cowell, ed., *The Jātaka*, vol. 1, translated by Robert Chalmers, Cambridge University Press, originally published 1895, reprinted 1957, 1969. Reprinted with permission of Cambridge University Press; (pp. 132–4) *The Dhammapada*, translated with notes by Nārada Thera, John Murray Publishers, Ltd; (pp. 173–9) B. Peter Harvey, *An Introduction to Buddhism: Teachings, History and Practices*, Cambridge University Press, 1990. Reprinted with permission of Cambridge University Press; (pp. 165–6) Robert K. Heinemann, 'This World and the Other Power: Contrasting Paths to Deliverance in Japan', in *The World of Buddhism: Buddhist Monks and Nuns in Society and Culture*, Facts on File Publications, © 1984 Thames and Hudson Ltd, London; (pp. 130–2) Christmas Humphries, ed., *The Wisdom of Buddhism*, Curzon Press Ltd, 1987. Reprinted by permission of the publisher; (pp. 134–5) *The Sutta-Nipāta*, translated by H. Saddhitissa, Curzon Press Ltd, 1985. Reprinted by permission of the publisher.

Jean Boisselier
was born, and lives, in Paris.
He holds doctorates in literature and Indian studies
and a doctorate *honoris causa* from Silpakorn
University in Bangkok, Thailand.
A former member of the
Ecole Française d'Extrême Orient,
he was curator of the Phnom Penh Museum
from 1950 to 1955 and in charge of
scientific research at the conservation department
of the Angkor monuments from 1953 to 1955.
Professor Boisselier was professor emeritus at the
Sorbonne University, in Paris, where he taught
before retiring in 1980 as chairman of the department
of South Asian and Southeast Asian studies.
A specialist in the art, archaeology and Buddhist
studies of India, Sri Lanka and Southeast Asia,
he is the author of eleven books.
Professor Boisselier has also conducted
numerous archaeological expeditions in
Cambodia, Vietnam, Sri Lanka
and, especially, in Thailand.

Translated by Carey Lovelace

First Published in the United Kingdom in 1994 by
Thames & Hudson Ltd, 181A High Holborn
London WC1V 7QX

Reprinted 1995, 2002

English translation © Thames & Hudson Ltd,
London, 1994

© 1993 Gallimard

British Library Cataloguing-in-Publication Data

A catalogue record for this book is available from
the British Library

ISBN 0–500–30047–X

Printed and bound in Italy
by Editoriale Lloyd, Trieste